Glee
TOTALLY UNOFFICIAL

The Ultimate Guide to the Smash-Hit High School Musical

Lisa Kidder

TRIUMPH
B O O K S

contents

Center

What Led Up To the Birth of *Glee*

Glee is a ground-breaking one-hour comedy musical television series unlike anything that has been seen on TV to date. The show's main character, Will Schuester, portrayed by Matthew Morrison, is a Spanish teacher at the fictional McKinley High in Lima, OH, who takes on the additional role of Glee Club director. "New Directions!" performance choir coach "Mr. Schu" leads his talented teens through the dramas and pitfalls of daily life, encouraging them to pour their energies into a healthy outlet—their singing performances. Though the history of fiction-based musicals is nothing new, this is the first time that we have seen it capture the loyalty of weekly TV viewers with such success.

One of the assumptions behind *Glee* is that those who participated in high school show choirs or "Glee Clubs" have not always been the

Stage

Photo by Charley Gallay/Stringer by Getty Images

most popular upper-echelon of teenage society. Perhaps one of the things that makes *Glee* so appealing is that it demonstrates that there's a little bit of geeky love of musical entertainment in all of us—jocks, cheerleaders, science whizzes, people with disabilities, shy kids, and rockers alike. A love for music and the desire to shine in the spotlight in some small way are things that most of us can share in common. It's this feeling that makes us want to cheer for the underdog characters of the show who are brave enough to put themselves on the line and sing with such heart.

Each *Glee* cast member has photos featuring their fingers in the shape of an "L" against their foreheads—the sign for "loser." Following the theme of the show, they have embraced this once derogatory symbol and claimed it as their own. Actress Amber Riley who plays Mercedes Jones described the motto as "Embrace your inner loser."

It's the show that everyone is talking about. *Glee* generated more Twitter social networking activity than any other television show in 2009, at 1.4 million Tweets. Ryan Murphy, Ian

Brennan, and Brad Falchuck are the three co-creators of the show. Originally envisioned as a movie, Brennan wrote a screenplay version of *Glee*, which Murphy suggested might make for interesting television. Within just the first few episodes, *Glee* managed to build a massive fan base proudly known as "gleeks."

The show's creator, Ryan Murphy, showed us that he was capable of creating something more light-hearted than his darkly captivating series *Nip/Tuck*. Never an idle moment, Murphy is busy in the film industry as well as TV. In addition to writing the screenplay for and directing the 2006 movie that was an adaptation of Augusten Burrough's book by the same title, *Running with Scissors*, Murphy also wrote the screenplay for and directed a movie about another bestselling book, *Eat, Pray, Love*, that will be released in 2010.

Glee may feature adolescent characters and show tune numbers, but don't be fooled by the seemingly innocent façade. Murphy's satirical and unusual interpretation of comedy and drama are still apparent throughout each episode. Dealing with edgy and subversive themes is something that has become a Ryan Murphy trademark. Some of the hot topics that the show has included are the

AND THE WINNER IS...

Still in the middle of its first season, *Glee* has already received numerous accolades and awards. Here is a list of a few of the achievements thus far:

2010 Golden Globe award for Best Comedy Series

2010 Golden Globe nomination for Best Actress (Lea Michele)

2010 Golden Globe nomination for Best Actor (Matthew Morrison)

2010 Golden Globe nomination for Best Supporting Actress (Jane Lynch)

2010 Screen Actor's Guild award for Best Ensemble in a Comedy Series

2010 People's Choice Award for Favorite New TV Comedy

2010 WGA Award (TV) nomination from the Writer's Guild of America for Best Comedy Series (Ian Brennan, Brad Falchuck, and Ryan Murphy)

2010 WGA Award (TV) nomination from the Writer's Guild of America for Best New Series (Ian Brennan, Brad Falchuk, and Ryan Murphy)

2010 Satellite Award for Best Television Series, Comedy, or Musical

2010 Satellite Award for Best Actor in a Series, Comedy, or Musical (Matthew Morrison)

2010 Satellite Award for Best Actress in a Series, Comedy, or Musical (Lea Michele)

2010 Satellite Award for Best Actress in a Supporting Role in a Series, Mini-Series, or Motion Picture Made for Television (Jane Lynch)

2010 Satellite Award nomination for Best Actor in a Supporting Role in a Series, Mini-Series, or Motion Picture Made for Television (Chris Colfer)

2009 Artios Award from the Casting Society of America for Outstanding Achievement in Casting for a television comedy pilot.

2009 Teen Choice Award nomination for Choice TV Breakout Show

2009 Teen Choice Award nomination for Choice TV Breakout Star: Female (Lea Michele)

2009 Teen Choice Award nomination for Choice TV Breakout Star: Male (Cory Monteith)

unplanned teenage pregnancy storyline, homosexuality, sexting (sexy texting), taking over-the-counter drugs to pep up the energy of musical numbers, lacing bake sale cupcakes with marijuana, lying, and scheming to get ahead.

Though some of the subjects are indisputably controversial, *Glee* manages to handle most of the sensitive themes realistically yet compassionately. One example is the male teenage homosexual character, Kurt Hummel, coming out to his conservative father. It was

a very big moment that was conveyed with both humor and parental love. Not every storyline has an immediate clean and happy ending though, such as is the case in the messy struggle between the cheerleader character, Quinn Fabray, and her parents who kicked her out of the house when they found out that she was pregnant.

Ultimately however, the general feel of the show is one that is uplifting. Drawing from his own experiences performing in musical theater during his youth in the Midwest, Murphy imparts

some of the optimism into the story line that being a part of something bigger can evoke. Murphy sees *Glee* as "a post-modern musical," not the type of production where people "suddenly burst into song," but rather one where the musical numbers are intended to be performances. While serving to further the plot of each episode, the songs are all done on stage, in rehearsals, or for the purpose of singing to someone about something. There are occasional exceptions that push the boundaries of this rule, such as in the "Acafellas" episode of *Glee*

AP Photo/Charles Sykes

American television in May 2009 following an episode of *American Idol*, hoping to draw in *Idol* fans with its performances featuring popular hits. The hook worked, but viewers had to be patient, since the second episode did not air until September 2009. During that long interlude, news articles and gossip blogs were busy speculating what might be in store for the series, while the *Glee* cast made appearances at Hot Topics stores in malls across the country. *Glee* also took a long hiatus in the middle of Season One, while cast

where Mercedes found herself fantasizing about singing the song "Bust Your Windows" or in the "Wheels" episode where Artie sings "Dancing with Myself," which begins and ends on stage, but also includes a sequence where he's wandering the halls and cafeteria singing, but nobody seems to notice him.

Straight from the beginning, *Glee* began by mixing it up. The first season of *Glee* featured a premier and a timeline that broke dramatically from the norm. The pilot episode debuted on

Photo by Michael Tran/FilmMagic

members made appearances at awards shows, worked hard filming upcoming episodes, and prepared for their next tour. The last nine episodes of Season One hit the TV screen in April 2010.

The success of shows such as *American Idol* and the movie *High School Musical* may have served as precedents for the general public acceptance of a show such as *Glee*. Being musicals featuring high school characters is where the similarities between *High School Musical* and *Glee* end, however. Glee has been described as the

Murphy sees *Glee* as "a postmodern musical," not the type of production where people "suddenly burst into song," but rather one where the musical numbers are intended to be performances.

"anti-*High School Musical*." Intended for a more mature audience, *Glee* is much more daring in the topics it tackles. Furthermore, it doesn't necessarily promise to tie up a clean and neat "happily ever after" for every character or

story line. Actor Cory Monteith who plays *Glee's* Finn Hudson had this to say about the comparison: "*High School Musical* fits inside of a very tidy box. It's a very specific tone. *Glee* is something of a satire. It takes apart that tone. It makes fun of itself."

Both *High School Musical* and *Glee* captured attention with their innovative performance numbers. Not to be outdone by *High School Musical's* creative basketball choreography, *Glee* features a number in the "Wheels" episode that has the cast performing in wheelchairs while singing "Proud Mary." Show creator Ryan Murphy admitted that he had never seen any of the *High School Musical* movies. With *Glee*, the traditional musical has transitioned from stage and the big screen to a weekly television series that can be enjoyed by teens and adults in the comfort of their own homes.

Another popular musical that featured high school

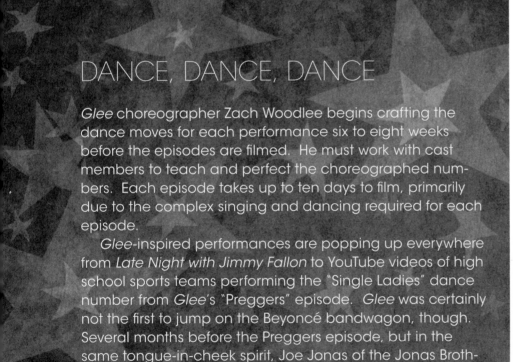

DANCE, DANCE, DANCE

Glee choreographer Zach Woodlee begins crafting the dance moves for each performance six to eight weeks before the episodes are filmed. He must work with cast members to teach and perfect the choreographed numbers. Each episode takes up to ten days to film, primarily due to the complex singing and dancing required for each episode.

Glee-inspired performances are popping up everywhere from *Late Night with Jimmy Fallon* to YouTube videos of high school sports teams performing the "Single Ladies" dance number from *Glee's* "Preggers" episode. *Glee* was certainly not the first to jump on the Beyoncé bandwagon, though. Several months before the Preggers episode, but in the same tongue-in-cheek spirit, Joe Jonas of the Jonas Brothers band released a promotional video in which he wore a black unitard and high heels and performed an awkward "Single Ladies" lip sync and dance number.

AP Photo/Matt Sayles

students was the 1978 film *Grease*, which was based upon a stage musical by the same name. In the movie *Grease*, the teenage star-crossed lover characters Danny Zuko and Sandy Olssen were played by actors John Travolta and Olivia Newton-John. The soundtrack incorporated both original songs as well as previous hits, yet it was the original songs that topped the charts. In Chapter Six of this book, you'll find more information about *Grease* star Olivia Newton-John's upcoming guest appearance on *Glee*.

The creators of *Glee* knew that the show could not be successful without the right casting. They went to great lengths to find actors who possessed what Ryan Murphy called the show business "triple threat," meaning performers who could sing, dance, and act.

Glee could be considered to fall into the category of a jukebox musical, which features a score of songs drawn from popular musical hits. *Mamma Mia!* is another example of a jukebox musical. From its stage production tours to the *Mamma Mia!* movie, the soundtrack was comprised entirely of songs by the group Abba and had audiences singing along to the familiar pop hits.

What sets *Glee* apart?

QUIZ: ARE YOU A GLEEK?

1 Do you watch every episode of *Glee*?

2 Is it programmed to record in the top 5 on your TiVo or DVR priority list?

3 Do you or did you not participate in a choir or musical program?

4 Can you name at least five characters or actors on the show?

5 Do you find yourself quoting lines from the show?

6 Do you check out *Glee* updates on MySpace, Facebook, or Twitter?

7 Do you purchase magazines or visit blogs for the express purpose of catching up on *Glee* gossip?

8 Do you identify with one or more of the characters on the show?

▶ **If you answered "yes" to three or more of the questions above: Congratulations, you are a gleek!**

▶ **If you answered "yes" to five or more of the questions above, you are a gleek maniac.**

▶ **If you answered yes to all of the questions above, you qualify to run for president of the *Glee* fan club.**

▶ **If you answered "yes" to less than three of the questions above, you are seriously missing out.**

Actress Lea Michele who stars as Rachel Berry said, "It's funny. It's smart. It's emotional, and then we have these incredible songs." In addition to America's growing love for musicals, the fanciful plot and optimistic attitude may also be a key to the show's success. Between the natural disasters, wars, and economic strain that make up so much of the news headlines, a bit of feel-good optimism on television is much appreciated. It is also one of the things that distinguishes the show from so many other things on TV today.

Murphy once commented, "There's so much on the air right now about people with guns, or sci-fi, or lawyers running around. This is a different genre, there's nothing like it on the air at the networks and cable. Everything's so dark in the world right now, that's why *Idol* worked. It's pure escapism." Actor Chris Colfer who plays character Kurt Hummel in the show described *Glee* as "a great show and what the world

Photo by Bob Levey/Getty Images

needs right now."

The ensemble cast of *Glee* play off each other to create a certain spark that ties the show together and keeps gleeks yearning for more. Remove any one member of the cast, and *Glee* would not have the same irresistible appeal. Chairman of 20th

Century Fox TV, Gary Newman said, "It was without a doubt the favorite casting process I've participated in."

Though many established actors and singers were proposed for the show, creator Ryan Murphy wanted to find the cast through a more organic process. They spent approximately three months travelling around the country listening to auditions for the various roles. Murphy weighed in on his opinion about the *Glee* ensemble cast with the statement, "We were so lucky that we found the whole cast. It seemed blessed from the beginning,

It's the show that everyone is talking about. *Glee* generated more Twitter social networking activity than any other television show in 2009, at 1.4 million tweets.

Photo: Mark Davis/PictureGroup) via AP IMAGES

the whole project."

Glee features great writing and original comedy, but it is the music that pulls it all together. At the 52nd Annual Grammy Awards, host Stephen Colbert jokingly referred to the Grammy Awards as "the highest honor the music industry can bestow... next to having your song covered by the cast of *Glee*."

Critics have speculated that the show's musical numbers would be more appealing if the actors sang rather than lip-synced their songs during the filming process. Though the talented actors do sing and record the songs for each episode, the formula has been to do the songs in a recording studio and then have the cast lip-sync to their own voices for the filming process.

In 2010, there is one episode in the works that will explore the use of original music, but there are no plans as of yet to make that an integral aspect of the show.

Murphy acknowledges that he found *American Idol* inspiring and thought that "the key is to do songs that people know and interpret them in a different and unusual way." Though the tunes are familiar to most, they are adapted in a way that makes their performance innovative and varied from the originals. They fit the theme and plot of each television episode, and the songs have made a splash off-screen as well as on-screen. *Glee* songs are available for download on iTunes immediately after the show is aired, and CD soundtracks for the show are available in stores.

The cast of *Glee* are not just lively and animated performers on the show. They

Actress Lea Michele who stars as Rachel Berry said, "It's funny. It's smart. It's emotional, and then we have these incredible songs."

PICK A SONG, ANY SONG . . .

The songs for *Glee* are chosen by show creator Ryan Murphy. He selects a blend of show tunes and popular radio hits, both modern and old, that fit the theme of each episode. Actor Mark Salling, who plays Puck, said that the musical numbers "are really an added bonus to help propel story lines."

PILOT EPISODE PLAY LIST:

"Don't Stop Believin'"
originally performed by Journey

"Rehab"
originally performed by Amy Winehouse

"On My Own"
originally from the stage musical *Les Miserables*

"Respect"
originally performed by Aretha Franklin

"Mr. Cellophane"
originally from the stage musical *Chicago*

"I Kissed a Girl"
originally performed by Katy Perry

"Sit Down, You're Rocking the Boat"
originally from the stage musical *Guys and Dolls*

"Can't Fight This Feeling"
originally performed by REO Speedwagon

have in fact been animated as cartoon images of their *Glee* characters in order to make guest appearances in the animated FOX series, *The Cleveland Show*. Each animated character makes a brief appearance to spotlight an example of their talent or utter a line or two that depicts the nature of their TV personalities.

While simultaneously being praised for its inclusion of a diverse set of characters that includes kids of different racial and ethnic backgrounds, different religious backgrounds, and a homosexual character, right alongside a character with a physical disability, *Glee* has received some criticism for casting a non-disabled person into a disabled role. Show creator Brad Falchuk commented on the deliberate intent to create a diverse set of characters for the show, while seeking out the best possible performers to play those roles. In reference to actor Kevin McHale who plays the paraplegic character Artie Abrams, Falchuk said, "It's hard to say no to someone that talented."

Creating a hit is not something that happens by accident. *Glee* has struck upon a winning combination that has successfully merged the concept of a traditional musical into a weekly television series with a plot and characters. This winning combination has millions of viewers, young and old, gladly identifying themselves as members of the gleek generation.

AP Photo/Paul Sakuma

The actors on *Glee* have received outstanding praise and prestigious entertainment industry awards for their charisma as an ensemble cast. There is something dynamic in ensemble acting that conveys a different tone than a show that features just one or two stars. It's not simply one individual who carries *Glee*, but rather the interaction of the cast as a whole.

Casting Directors Robert Ulrich, Eric Dawson, and Carol Kritzer deserve a round of applause for finding and casting this unique group of actors, who are not only multi-talented, but who lend so much to the overall flavor and appeal of the show. Always in demand for his skills as a casting director, Robert Ulrich has been responsible for assembling more than just the cast of *Glee*. He worked with Ryan Murphy in casting both *Nip/Tuck* and *Popular*, and he has also cast the TV shows *Caprica*, *Battlestar Galactica*, *The Mentalist*, *Saving Grace*,

Drop Dead Diva, Eastwick, CSI: Crime Scene Investigation, CSI: Miami, Eureka, Supernatural, Everwood, Felicity, and many more.

The cast of *Glee* refer to each other as family. Not only do they spend long days together on the set filming episodes for the show, as well as in dance rehearsals and in the recording studio, but they also spend much of their free time together as well. They've been seen at restaurants having lunch and dinner together. They've been spotted in pairs or in groups at clubs or simply hanging out. They call and text each other when they have news to share.

What did they do before coming to *Glee*? Are they anything like their characters in real life? This chapter will take a closer look at the actors who portray your favorite *Glee* characters. It's their unique talent that really sells the characters and makes them believable.

MATTHEW MORRISON

as Will Schuester

Matthew Morrison portrays the role of Spanish teacher Will Schuester, the intrepid leader of McKinley High's Glee Club. "Mr. Schu," as he is known to his students, has fond memories of participating in the Glee Club back when he attended McKinley High School, and he invests his time and energy into making sure that his glee students are able to harness this worthwhile form of creative expression.

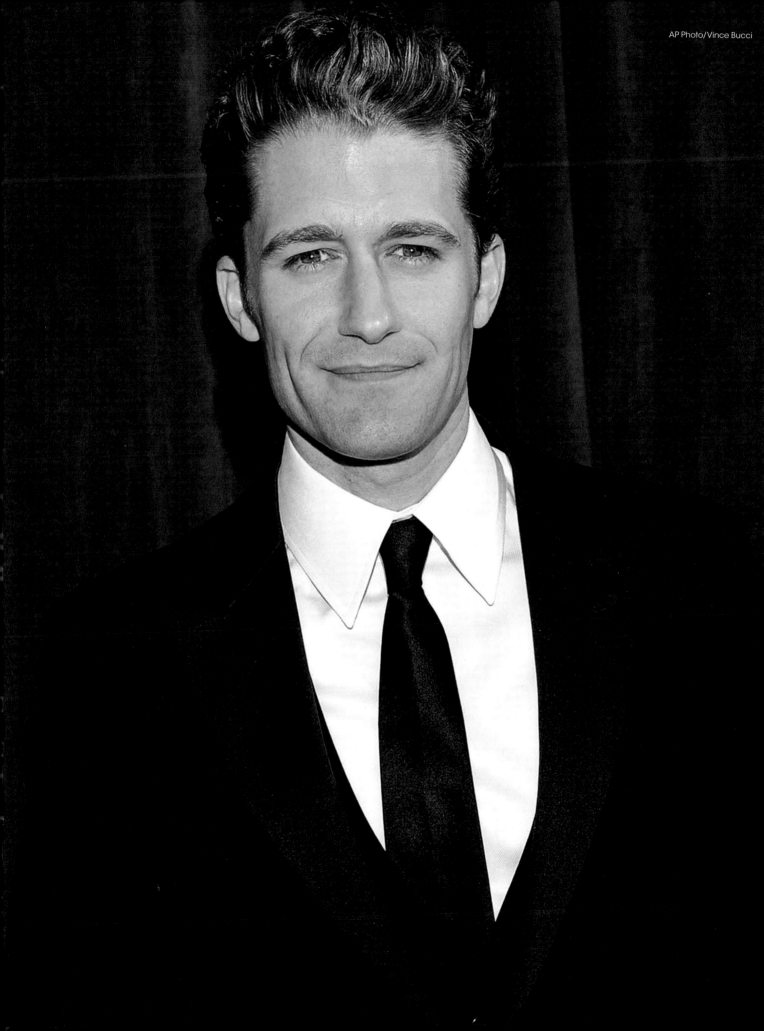

AP Photo/Jeff Christensen

then, I think there's a show that's just so fresh and you can't compare it to anything like a cop show or a lawyer show. It's its own thing and that's what makes the show so appealing. And there's so much optimism at a time we need it. It's a true underdog story and we've all been the underdog at some point in our lives."

It comes as no surprise that actor Matthew Morrison has a background in musical theater. Prior to landing the role of Will Schuester in *Glee*, Morrison already had a successful career as a Broadway actor. In addition to playing a member of the singing and dancing ensemble cast in the Broadway version of *Footloose*, Morrison also played a role in the stage revival of the *Rocky Horror Show*. Coincidentally, in both musicals, Morrison served as a replacement to an original cast member.

Repeating the same combination of talent and good timing, Morrison landed his first major starring role in the spotlight after serving as an understudy once again, when he portrayed the role of the hunky teenage heart-throb, Link Larkin, in the long-running Broadway adaptation of John Water's *Hairspray*. *Hairspray* is a musical about teenagers who decide to integrate the dancers on a segregated television show during the

So what does Matthew Morrison think of Will Schuester? Apparently, he can relate to his fictional character very well. In an interview with *Parade*, he said, "If I could have written a part for myself, this would have been it. It showcases everything I've trained for, and it's the kind of teaching job I could easily have wound up doing myself in real life."

When asked his opinion about why *Glee* resonates so well with viewers, Morrison replied in an interview with TVGuide.com, "It's such an original show. Every now and height of the civil rights movement. Like *Glee*, *Hairspray* features a diverse mixture of teenage characters, many of whom overcome the odds as underdogs fighting for a cause. Morrison received an Outer Critics Award nomination for Best Featured Actor in a Musical for his work in *Hairspray*.

Morrison's Broadway acting credits also include playing the role of Thad Lapin in the Broadway play A *Naked Girl on the Appian Way*. His performance in the stage musical *10 Million Miles* earned him a Drama Desk nomination for Outstanding Actor in a Musical. His most recent Broadway appearance was playing the role of Lt. Joseph Cable in a revival of the classic Rodgers and Hammerstein musical *South Pacific*. He left *South Pacific* in January 2009 in order to begin filming *Glee* in February 2009.

Perhaps Morrison's most notable achievement to date as a theater professional came when he received a Tony Award nomination for Best Performance by a Featured Actor in a Musical for his portrayal of Fabrizio Nacarelli in *The Light in the Piazza*, a musical adaptation of a novel by Elizabeth Spencer. This role also earned him another Drama Desk nomination for Outstanding Actor in a musical, along with an Outer Critics Circle Award nomination for Best Featured Actor in a Musical.

Morrison's movie credits include *Dan in Real Life*, *Music and Lyrics*, and *I Think I Love My Wife*, and he also starred in the made-for-TV movie *Once Upon a Mattress* with Carol Burnett and Tracy Ullman. No stranger to television, Morrison made guest appearances on TV shows that included *The Ghost Whisperer*, *Sex and the City*, *Hack*, *CSI: Miami*, and *Law and Order: Criminal Intent*. He also had a brief stint as a cast member in the soap opera *As the World Turns*.

All of Morrison's stage, TV, and film experience before *Glee* did not add up to the fame that he has received since being cast as Will Schuester. Morrison commented that, "It's crazy the amount of people that just watch this show. More people watched the pilot of *Glee* than my entire ten years on Broadway in New York."

Morrison was born at Fort Ord Army Base in California and has referred to himself as an "army brat." The son of a nurse mother and a midwife father, he developed his love for acting at a very young age. He attended a theater camp as a child, and he performed in

AP Photo/Charles Sykes

EVERYBODY CUT LOOSE, FOOTLOOSE

Morrison's role in *Glee*'s "Acafellas" was not his first attempt at a boy band. He sang in the satirical mock boy band Fresh Step for "The Late Show with David Letterman." Fresh Step was comprised of cast members from the Broadway musical *Footloose*.

Morrison also tried his hand at a more traditional version of a boy band as one of the original four performers of LMNT (pronounced "element"), though he wasn't with the band for long. In fact, he quit before they released their first full-length CD in order to continue his Broadway acting career.

a children's theater show titled *The Herdman's Go to Camp*. Morrison remained focused on his dream throughout his life. He auditioned for placement into the Orange County High School of the Arts, where he was accepted and attended high school. Morrison continued to perform in musical theater and plays throughout school, but he wasn't quite one of the *Glee*-type underdogs during his days as a student. In fact, he was school president.

He played soccer, dated the homecoming queen, and was voted prom king.

In 2008, Morrison returned to the Orange County High School of the Arts to help out with their annual fundraiser, where he performed alongside students in a school production of *Moulin Rouge*. Heather Stafford, the Director of the Integrated Arts Conservatory at Orange County High School of the Arts, had this to say about Morrison: "The students just adored him. He's a very good example of how you need to put 120 percent of yourself into your work."

Morrison's singing and dancing skills are no mere coincidence. He has worked hard throughout his life and dedicated himself to pursuing his goals. He developed his singing and acting skills, and he took ballet, tap, and jazz dance classes. To further hone his craft, Morrison attended the prestigious Tisch School of the Arts at New York University where he studied musical theater, vocal performance, and dance. However, he got agent representation and dropped out of NYU so that he could go to auditions and spend time pursuing his acting career as opposed to going to classes.

Celebrity and fame were not a foregone conclusion for actor Matthew Morrison. Before landing on Broadway, he worked at The Gap in New York City to make ends meet, while he continued to seek out acting roles.

Willing to use his talents to give back to the community, Morrison once lent his time and toned physique to perform in *Broadway Bares 18: Wonderland*, an AIDS-related fundraising charity benefit. Morrison stripped down to a pair of colorful comic underwear and danced to "The Humpty Dance" by Digital Underground.

SAY ANYTHING . . .

The combination of writing talent and acting has resulted in the delivery of some very memorable lines from the show. Here are some of the favorites from *Glee* character Will Schuester, as uttered by Matthew Morrison:

"Athletes are performers, just like singers and dancers." (From the "Preggers" episode.)

"I'd love to play 'This is Your Life,' but Lord Google demands my attention." (From "The Rhodes Not Taken" episode.)

"A mash-up is when you take two songs and mash them together to make an even richer explosion of musical expression." (From the "Vitamin D" episode.)

"Sue Sylvester, you're going to have to pry those F's from my cold, dead hands." (From the "Throwdown" episode.)

"You're all minorities. You're in the Glee Club. There are only twelve of you, and all you have is each other." (From the "Throwdown" episode.)

"Welcome to the Glee Club's first official 'Diva-Off.' Let's get this party started!" (From the "Wheels" episode.)

Morrison was once asked in an interview if he had the opportunity to date any celebrities since embracing his own new-found *Glee* fame. Although he didn't own up to any actual relationships, he commented, "...I was in New York doing a workshop for a new musical with Jessica Biel, this beautiful Argentinean actor Mía Maestro, and Salma Hayek. I really like smart women, and [Hayek] is really brilliant. We went out to lunch a couple times. We had great conversations all week, and

I would have no shame in perpetuating it. I'll be John Wayne's grandson! You know, his real name was Marion Morrison—and if you look at pictures of both of us, it's quite uncanny."

What does Matthew Morrison do for hobbies? He's been known to thrive on a bit of adrenaline even when he is not performing live or on TV. He has tried his hand at a few extreme sports such as skydiving and boxing. He's a runner and a cyclist, and he also plays an occasional round of

is written out word-for-word? The scenes between Matthew Morrison and Jane Lynch, who plays Coach Sue Sylvester, have resulted in quite a bit of spontaneous action and dialogue ending up in the final cut. Morrison once commented in an interview, "We go in with our lines, but with Jane and I, they really let us go. A lot of what they keep for the scene is our ad-lib. We have a lot of great stuff together. Those scenes are so much fun to do, except I have to try not to laugh."

One of the most memorable *Glee* performances featuring Matthew Morrison was in the "Showmance" episode where Morrison rapped the Kanye West song "Gold Digger." He showed us that he was not only a diverse singer, but that he was an amazing dancer, too. Morrison rapped and showed his moves once again in the "Mash-Up" episode to the "Bust a Move" tune by Young MC.

> ## "We go in with our lines, but with Jane and I, they really let us go. A lot of what they keep for the scene is our ad-lib. We have a lot of great stuff."

she, like, cried when she had to say good-bye to me. It was a great romance without having any real romance." When asked who was his first celebrity crush, Morrison replied, "Tiffani-Amber Thiessen from *Saved by the Bell*. I loved her."

It was once rumored that Matthew Morrison was the grandson of cowboy western movie star John Wayne. When asked if it was indeed a fact, Morrison replied, "Oh, God! That is just a rumor, but

golf when he has the time.

What does Matthew Morrison think of *Glee*? It sounds like he has a lot of fun filming with his ensemble cast of co-stars and appreciates the energy and enthusiasm both on set and off. "There's a certain amount of camp involved in the show," Morrison said. "The reason we get away with so much stuff is because we don't take ourselves too serious."

How much of the dialogue is ad-libbed and how much

Capitalizing on his singing talents, Morrison is in the process of recording an original album for Mercury Records. When asked to describe the album, Morrison commented, "It's going to be different. I would consider it a classier Justin Timberlake album. It's going to be me and a big orchestra, but also with beats." His debut CD will be available in the fall of 2010.

JANE LYNCH
as Sue Sylvester

Actress Jane Lynch plays McKinley High's hostile and narcissistic cheerleading coach, Sue Sylvester. Lynch's portrayal of Sue adds a spark to the show that has fans begging for more.

Lynch claims that she was immediately in love with the role of Sue Sylvester and laughs out loud when she reads every script. She enjoys the challenge of constantly trying to walk that "fine line between deliciousness and heinousness" when playing the part.

Jane Lynch with cast mate Dianna Agron during the 67th Annual Golden Globe Awards.

The outspoken and belligerent character of Sue Sylvester can be a cathartic role to play. "I always say when I put on that track suit I have a license to say anything I want," Lynch said. "I think it's probably very good therapy, because I'm a much nicer person at home because I get it all out at work, and that kind of contemptuousness and heinous behavior is just very shallowly below the surface for me so it's kind of nice. I don't have to dig deep for it, but it's great I can do it there on the set and then I don't have to do it at home." No doubt her fiancée, Dr. Lara Embry, appreciates that fact. The two plan to tie the knot in May 2010.

Lynch's character, Coach Sue, is not always brutally scathing. In the "Wheels" episode of *Glee*, we got to see Lynch play her softer side, as we learned about Sylvester's sister with Down's Syndrome who lives in a professional care facility home. Lynch played the part with understated compassion.

Lynch has become known for her straight-faced, deadpan delivery of comedic lines and for playing sarcastic characters with a dry sense of humor. Though the dialogue that is written for her or that she ad-libs herself is often outrageous, she is able to communicate as much with a single look as she can with her words.

Growing up in Illinois, Lynch performed in choir during high school, though she struggled with getting parts in school plays. Lynch said of her high school days, "I was one of those happy travelers and really didn't stay in one group. I kind of got around without getting humiliated and was in a little bit of everything."

On *The Bonnie Hunt Show*, Lynch talked about her high school days performing in the school choir. "In the choir room, it was like the great equalizer, music," Lynch said. "When you get a bunch of different kids from different

SAY ANYTHING . . .

The dialogue for the character Sue Sylvester is ripe with so many shocking and hilarious phrases, that it was difficult to narrow down a selection of favorites amongst the many gems. Though they do not have the same impact on paper as they do being delivered by Lynch, here are a few lines that really stand out:

"You think this is hard? Try being water boarded. That's hard." (Opening line of the pilot episode.)

"So here's the deal. You do with your depressing little group of kids what I did with my wealthy elderly mother: Euthanize it." (To Will Schuester in the "Showmance" episode.)

"If I was out to get you, I'd have you pickling in a mason jar on my shelf by now." (To Will Schuester in the "Preggers" episode.)

"You know, when I heard that Sandy wanted to write himself into a scene as Queen Cleopatra, I was aroused, then furious." (From "The Rhodes Not Taken" episode.)

"Glee Club. Every time I try to destroy that clutch of scab-eating mouth breathers, it only comes back stronger like some sexually ambiguous horror movie villain." (From the "Vitamin D" episode.)

"In fact, I like minorities so much, I'm thinking of moving to California to become one." (From the "Throwdown" episode.)

AP Photo/Tammie Arroyo

Photo by: Paul Drinkwater/NBCU Photo Bank via AP Images

Lynch and *Glee* creator Ryan Murphy crossed paths a few years ago when Lynch worked with Murphy on a 2001 episode of *Popular*. The episode titled "I Know What You Did Last Spring Break" was a loosely-based satirical spoof of the movie *I Know What You Did Last Summer*, in which Lynch played guest character Susie Klein, a travel agent turned vengeful serial killer.

groups within the high school, the social hierarchy gets kind of flipped around. Music is the great equalizer where everybody is the same and you're all working toward one kind of beautiful thing." Lynch and Hunt talked during the show about how *Glee* conveys this sentiment as an underlying theme.

Lynch studied acting and theatre at Illinois State University and continued on to receive her Master of Fine Arts graduate degree from Cornell University. She also

plays guitar and has been actively committed to her acting career since college.

With a background in theater, Lynch starred as Carol Brady in the long running play, *The Real Live Brady Bunch*, which had a loyal cult following. The cast members in the play re-enacted episodes from the original *Brady Bunch* television series.

Though she did not sing on *Glee* in the first portion of Season One, she is no novice to musical performance. She recorded a peppy pop song titled "On Hold 4 You" for the movie *A Cinderella Story*, in which she played wicked step-mother Dominique Blatt. Prior to that, Lynch also starred in the Christopher Guest movie *A Mighty Wind*, a mockumentary

about folk singers, in which she sang and played guitar several times throughout the film.

Lynch starred in another Christopher Guest movie, *Best in Show*, in which she played a tenacious show dog owner, and in Guest's movie *For Your Consideration*, she played an entertainment news journalist. In these Christopher Guest movies, Lynch was left much to her own devices to create and improvise her characters. This sort of improvisational acting really stretches the boundaries for an actor, and Lynch is a master of it.

"It kind of makes me more aggressive and I demand more from myself when I do a script at show," said Lynch of her previous improvisational acting experience. "I see it as being

"I think if you can do comedy, you can do anything because you can pick up the ironies in life better. It takes a little more investigation into your own heart with comedy."

creative. My character process, I think, is probably a little more creative than if I hadn't done that kind of work where I had to create something out of whole cloth. That's why I think I can push things maybe to the Nth degree, because I'm used to doing that from having to make it up on my own."

Lynch has received great praise from critics for her part in *Glee*. *Los Angeles Times* Television Critic, Mary McNamara had this to say about Lynch: "Lynch alone makes *Glee* worth watching. All by her lonesome, Sue summons up what is most feared, loathed, and secretly admired in a high school teacher-coach, running the Cheerios, a high-pressure, high-performing cheerleading squad, like an East German gymnastic team."

Will we ever get to hear her sing on *Glee*? According to the numerous show spoilers that abound throughout the media, every indication is that the answer to that question is a resounding "Yes!" We can look forward to hearing Lynch sing in the second half of Season One.

Already an established actress prior to coming to *Glee*, Lynch has starred in movies, appeared on dozens of television shows, and even written and starred in her own play titled *Oh Sister, My Sister!* As a woman who seems on top of the world at the moment,

where does she go from here? Lynch admits that in addition to playing the role of Sue Sylvester, she would very much enjoy directing an episode of *Glee* at some point in the future. Other than that, she intends to take life as it comes, claiming that she "never makes decisions carefully." As funny off screen as on, Lynch is always ready

POP QUIZ

In January 2010, Lynch made a guest appearance on the TV show *Who Wants to Be a Millionaire* to ask the $10,000 celebrity question featuring *Glee*. The question was:

"The pilot episode of *Glee* memorably concludes with the cast performing 'Don't Stop Believin',' a 1981 power ballad by what band?
   A. REO Speedwagon
   B. Survivor
   C. Journey
   D. The Cars"
True gleeks (and Journey fans) know that the answer is, of course, "C. Journey."

with an unexpected quip and often adds off-the-cuff humor to her interviews. At the Golden Globe awards, Jane Lynch announced to a reporter on the red carpet that she was carrying a tampon in her purse. On *The Bonnie Hunt Show*, she described a humorous memory on the red carpet in which her elderly mother ran over to actress Meryl Streep to introduce herself.

Lynch once commented, "I think if you can do comedy, you can do anything because you can pick up the ironies in life better. It takes a little more investigation into your own heart with comedy."

How does Lynch feel about her part in the making of *Glee*? "I feel like there's nothing better than being satisfied with your work and feeling really good about your work."

In an interview conducted around the same time as beginning work on the *Glee* pilot episode, Lynch was asked if she'd like to do more television rather than movies. She indicated that she's done a lot of movies and she's done a fair amount of television every season, but often in guest appearance roles. She went on to say that what she would really like would be a television series, "I hope that a pilot I do gets picked up. I would love to hang my hat somewhere for a while." It looks like with *Glee*, Lynch got her wish.

DIANNA AGRON

as Quinn Fabray

Dianna Agron plays *Glee* character Quinn Fabray, the popular and sometimes scathing blonde cheerleader whose boyfriend is McKinley High's quarterback, Finn Hudson. Despite the fact that she is president of the Christ Crusader's Celibacy Club, one of the major storylines running throughout *Glee* Season One was her unplanned pregnancy. Agron (pronounced "A-gron" with a long "A") says that she was nothing

AP Photo/Vince Bucci

Dianna Agron, left, and Lea Michele, pose together backstage after the cast of *Glee* won the award for best comedy ensemble at the 16th Annual Screen Actors Guild awards.

like her character, Quinn, in high school. However, she says that part of the fun of playing the role is because she is so different. Willing to work hard, Agron juggled many different projects and activities during school.

Even though she spent 20 hours a week practicing and teaching dance, Agron still managed to maintain good grades and take honors classes in high school. She also participated in theater and held down a job while she was still a student.

Agron knew from the time she was a kid that she wanted to be a performer. Her first audition was for the role of Dorothy in *The Wizard of Oz* when she was in the fifth grade. Discovering her dream at such a young age, she had this to say about pursuing her ambition: "Finding out that I could incorporate acting, singing, and dancing [in a job] was novel to me as a kid. I did musical theater throughout school and that paved the way."

Though she was not a cheerleader herself during her high school days, this is not the first time that Agron has played a competitive and territorial cheerleader. In Season Two of the television series *Heroes*, Agron played a recurring character named Debbie Marshall, the head cheerleader and nemesis of mainstay character Claire Bennett. When Claire had enough of being pushed around and snubbed by Agron's character, Debbie, the healing hero played a prank on her adversary that resulted in humiliating Debbie and getting her suspended from school.

Agron was also featured in various guest roles on several other television series, including *Veronica Mars*, *Drake & Josh*, *CSI: NY*, and *Numb3rs*.

SAY ANYTHING . . .

Agron's character on the show, Quinn Fabray, began as a stereotypical high school mean girl. Over time, Agron was able to show a softer side, as her character was forced to tackle some larger problems in life. Her most memorable lines on the show reflect that her character cares greatly about popularity and status and also that she is beginning to learn who her true friends really are. Here are some of the best of Dianna Agron's lines as Quinn Fabray, to date:

"People think you're gay now, Quinn. And you know what that makes me? Your big gay beard."
(From the "Showmance" episode.)

"Are you a moron? We're not naming our baby 'Drizzle.'"
(From the "Throwdown" episode.)

"This is a disaster. Our reputation as McKinley High's 'It' couple is in serious jeopardy if we don't find some way to be cool again, Finn." (From the "Mash-Up" episode.)

"Status is like currency. When your bank account is full, you can get away with doing just about anything."
(From the "Mash-Up" episode.)

"Somewhere in that pea brain of yours is a man. Access him, and tell him to prove to me that I chose the right guy to have a baby with." (From the "Wheels" episode.)

"It would be good for the school, showing everyone that appearances don't matter. Sometimes people have to deal with a little adversity. I learned that in Glee Club."
(From the "Mattress" episode.)

AP Photo/Jennifer Graylock

Born in the South in Savannah, Georgia, Agron moved to California when she was young. Her father was a manager for Hyatt, and Agron spent part of her childhood living in a luxury San Francisco hotel.

Influenced by films such as *Singin' in the Rain* and *Funny Face*, Agron performed in musical theater while she was in school. She attended Burlingame High School in the northern California San Francisco Bay area. After graduating from high school, Agron moved to Los Angeles in order to pursue her dream of being an actress.

Agron and fellow *Glee* cast member, Lea Michele, have lived as roommates in L.A. They would sometimes have their castmates over to their place to hang out off set. Agron enjoys cooking at home, but she doesn't like her foods to touch on her plate. Unlike her character on the show, Agron is Jewish rather than Christian.

In an MTV interview, Agron reported that she likes unusual pets. She was in the process of preparing a salt water tank so that she could buy an octopus for a pet. It's a long process to prepare a tank for a high maintenance pet like an octopus, and they have to be separated from other fish so that they don't eat them for lunch.

Agron thinks that volunteering is a cool way to spend your time. She suggested that it's a good way to meet other people while helping people in need.

For her *Glee* audition, Agron was so nervous that she had to sit in her car for several minutes and work up the courage to actually go

THE MIGHTY QUINN

Expanding beyond the boundaries of television acting, Agron has already written and sold a screenplay titled *A Fuschia Elephant*. The screenplay is based upon a male character who has a real problem saying the three simple words "I love you." Agron's acting, singing, dancing, and writing talents, combined with her drive and ambition to go after what she wants, make it clear that this young actress is much more than just the character she plays.

Agron appears as comfortable in high couture fashion as she is in her Cheerios uniform. In addition to her growing collection of elegant gowns worn on the red carpets of various awards shows, Agron also modeled Versace, Armani and Chanel for *Interview* magazine.

We can expect to see Agron make appearances in several upcoming movies. *The Romantics* is an aptly named romantic comedy that played at the Sundance Film Festival in January 2010. In this movie about a group of friends with a past who reunite at a wedding, Agron plays Minnow, the younger sister of the bride-to-be. In a film from a very different type of genre, Agron plays a part in *The Hunters*, a horror movie about a group of town outsiders who hunt and kill their fellow citizens for sport. Agron also has a role in the film *Bold Native*, a movie about an animal rights activist who takes his convictions to an extreme level as a suspected terrorist.

The movie that will perhaps make the biggest splash is the upcoming musical *Burlesque* with Christina Aguilera and Cher.

inside. Fox casting directors liked what they saw, but asked her to make a few changes before coming back for a second round of auditions. At the last minute, she was asked to straighten her hair for the call-back, and short on time, Agron quickly bought a straightening iron at a store and went into a Starbuck's bathroom to work on smoothing her locks. She sang "Fly Me to the Moon" by Frank Sinatra for her audition song.

Agron told fans at the 2009 Comic Con in San Diego, CA, that it all happened very fast. She was the last person cast for the show. She auditioned on a

be found at felldowntherabbithole.tumblr.com, is titled "You can call me Charlie," and though she talks about everything from her favorite music to what her day was like, she doesn't openly advertise all over the page that she is writing the posts. The entire blog has an almost surreal quality, indicating

AP Photo/Vince Bucci

She auditioned on a Wednesday. She got a call to come back in for a second audition on that Friday, where she was told that she was to start work on the show two days later.

Wednesday. She got a call to come back in for a second audition on that Friday, where she was told that she was to start work on the show two days later.

Agron's interests stray toward the dark and mysterious. She likes pirates, skulls, witchcraft, and gargoyles. She admitted to talk show host George Lopez that she has a love for the beauty and tranquility of cemeteries. Acting, singing, and dancing are not Agron's only creative pursuits. She also writes poetry. On her blog, Agron shared a poem she wrote in her journal one day while visiting a set of catacombs in Europe.

Agron's blog, which can

that Agron's interests themselves are rather eccentric and artistic. Her posts span a wide range of topics—art, music, the work of Tim Burton, skulls, gargoyles, fiction, and poetry, just to name a few.

Agron believes that you have to take risks and go after what you want in life. It certainly has served her well. She had this advice to offer on the subject, "The challenge is getting off your couch and doing it, making the conscious decision to put your [ideas] into motion." She went on to say, "You can always find a reason not to try. But unless you become fully invested, you'll never know what could

CORY MONTEITH

as Finn Hudson

Cory Monteith plays Finn Hudson, McKinley High School's popular quarterback and first Glee Club member from the "popular" crowd. Though adorably clueless about some things, his sincerity and earnestness allow others to be comfortable following his lead. Gary Newman, Chairman of 20th Century Fox TV, referred to the character of Finn as "the greatest casting challenge" on the show.

Ryan Murphy and Kevin Riley both felt strongly that the role of Finn needed to be a genuine "guy's guy" football player type while still being a believable underdog. Add those qualities to the requirement that the actor who portrayed Finn would also need to be able to sing, dance, and act, and it is easy to see how all of these factors combined added up to a difficult role to fill.

Monteith was one of the only actors in the cast of Glee who did not have previous singing or dancing experience. Reluctant to sing on his initial audition video, he chose to play the drums instead, using a collection of glasses, plastic storage containers, and unsharpened pencils as drumsticks. Impressed by Monteith's impromptu drumming, the creators of Glee decided to write Finn as a drummer into the storyline.

Of course, the Glee casting directors wanted to hear Monteith sing, too, so for another audition tape, Monteith told fans at the 2009 Comic Con in San Diego, CA, that he sang REO Speedwagon, though he was uncertain whether or not that tape was ever viewed by FOX executives. Whether it was his rendition of REO Speedwagon or his unique drumming skills that garnered him a phone call, we may never know, but the end result was that he received a call telling him that casting director Robert Ulrich and show creator Ryan Murphy would like to see him in person for a test audition. Monteith made the twenty hour drive from Vancouver to Los Angeles in a car by himself. "Just me, the soundtrack from

SAY ANYTHING . . .

Monteith plays Finn Hudson with a blend of honesty, naiveté, leadership skills, and pure teenage boy that makes Finn Hudson one of the most endearing characters on the show. Here are a few of the ultimate Finn Hudson lines from Glee:

"No, I can't do the solo Mr. Schu. I'm still learning how to walk and sing at the same time."
(From the "Showmance" episode.)

"I'm still on the fence about the celibacy club. I mean, I only joined to get into Quinn Fabray's pants."
(From the "Showmance" episode.)

"I got this at the school library. Do you know that you can just borrow books from there? All of them, except for the encyclopedias." (From the "Preggers" episode.)

"I know how lucky I am—captain of the football team, glee stud. I know I should be excited about Quinn. She's hot, popular, and she's carrying my baby and all, but I can't get Rachel out of my head. She kind of freaks me out in a *Swim Fan* kind of way, but she can really sing, and her body is smoking, if you're not into boobs."
(From the "Vitamin D" episode.)

"I don't think any one decision makes your life, unless you accidentally invent some kind of zombie virus or something." (From the "Mash-Up" episode.)

"We can't do this without you, Mr. Schu. Hell, we probably can't do it with you." (From the "Mattress" episode.)

"Look, all that we have going for us is that we believe in ourselves and what we're singing about. If we can show the judges that, we might have a shot at this thing."
(From the "Sectionals" episode.)

Rent, and *Billy Joel's Greatest Hits*," he told Q TV of his hurried drive to his test audition. He was actually practicing in the car and trying to figure out which song to sing because he had never before sung in front of others for a performance.

For that call-back appearance, Monteith showed up to find roughly 25 other guys, with a similar look to his, waiting to audition for the same part. Fortunately, he worked up the courage to sing in person. He chose to sing "Honesty" by Billy Joel. He was invited back again for another test, where he sang the same song again, this time for more than twenty FOX network executives. After his test in person at FOX, he received a call approximately half an hour later telling him that he got the job.

When asked about how challenging it has been to sing and dance on a show with no real experience in those areas prior to starting work on *Glee*, Monteith had this to say, "It's been a great opportunity to learn how to sing and dance. I've never done anything like this before." He went on to elaborate, "It's been very challenging to perform with talented, seasoned Broadway performers." Overall, he feels that it has been a very challenging yet rewarding process that has really pushed him to expand his skills as an actor.

A drummer since the age

of seven, Monteith also played a drummer on MTV's series *Kaya*. The show was about a band with a lead singer by the name of Kaya, who was Monteith's fictional ex-girlfriend. In this television series, Monteith played the character of

CANADIAN PRIDE

Canadian Monteith was born in Calgary, Alberta, but spent several years of his youth in Victoria, British Columbia, eventually moving to Vancouver where he got his start in acting. He moved to Los Angeles in order to work on *Glee*, but he seems at home on the southern California beaches where he likes to skinboard and practice surfing. He also has the mountain ski resorts of Mammoth and Big Bear conveniently located not too far away, in case he wants to keep up on his snowboarding skills, too. However, in many ways, Monteith's heart is still in Canada. He's very proud of the fact that he is Canadian, and he returned to his former home of Vancouver for the opening ceremonies of the 2010 Winter Olympics in Februrary.

Gunner, a guy with heart, who played alongside Kaya as they navigated the road to music fame and all the pressures that came along with it.

From what we have seen so far in his public appearances, Monteith seems to fit Finn's "good guy" image in many ways. He says that he doesn't drink alcohol, and he appears to stay pretty low-key and true to himself despite his new-found fame. "I am what I am," said Monteith in his matter-of-fact way.

Though Monteith did not finish high school, he did work at a variety of jobs since leaving school. Before becoming a full-time actor, a few examples of the types of jobs he tried on for size include working at WalMart as a greeter, working in construction, changing oil, changing tires, being a taxi driver as well as a school bus driver, making phone calls as a telemarketer, and washing cars. One thing that this mixed bag of odd jobs has taught him was how to adjust and be versatile. He says that he's "always been that transient chameleon, doing whatever I have to do to get myself by...

It kind of makes you a bit of a quick study later in life. You kind of learn quickly how to adapt to any situation."

Monteith's acting resume includes a long list of television credits prior to *Glee*. On *Kyle XY*, he appeared in multiple episodes in which he played Charlie Tanner, the popular but not always loyal boyfriend to Amanda, the character who later became Kyle's girlfriend after she and Charlie broke up. Monteith appeared in this recurring guest role throughout Season One of *Kyle XY*.

In the popular science fiction television series *Stargate SG-1*, Monteith appeared in a self-spoofing episode in which he played a young version of SG-1 Lt. Colonel Cameron Mitchell. He also had a guest role in an episode of the spin-off series, *Stargate Atlantis*, in which he played a Genii military private.

Monteith's television experience also includes parts in *Smallville*, *Supernatural*, and *Flash Gordon*. He has been featured in several movies as well. He played roles in three full feature-length thrillers, *Whisper, Final Destination 3,*

"It's been a great opportunity to learn how to sing and dance. I've never done anything like this before."

The cast of *Glee* play a game of musical chairs on the set of MTV's *It's On with Alexa Chung.*

and *The Invisible*, as well as the mystery short film *Gone.* He also appeared in a more light-hearted film, *Deck the Halls.* His first experience in a more prominent starring role came in the form of the made-for-television movie, *Hybrid.* In this film, Monteith played the main character, Aaron Scates, a young blind man who received the eyes of a wolf in an experimental transplant surgery. The result was that he also developed some very wolf-like tendencies.

Monteith once auditioned for the Disney film *Sky High*, a movie about a high school for kids with super powers. He says that it was his most embar-rassing audition of his career because he got so nervous that he forgot his lines. Even when they told him that he was allowed to read from the script, he was still so nervous that he could barely utter a word.

In an interview for Canada's Q TV, Monteith talked about how he never would have predicted that his break out role as an actor would have included singing and dancing. He said that his biggest area of growth through the whole process has probably been just learning to develop enough confidence to sing out loud to the best of his ability. With no background in musical theater, it was fellow *Glee* cast member,

GLEE CLUB INSPIRATION

The cast members of *Glee* have been told many times by fans that the show has inspired them to join Glee Club or even start up Glee Clubs that didn't previously exist at their schools. Monteith said, "That's one of our favorite things to hear. When we hear kids come up and say 'We're start-ing a Glee Club because of the show,' we're like... What's better than that, than inspiring kids?"

CORY MONTEITH AS FINN HUDSON

Lea Michele, who took him to his first Broadway show, *Rock of Ages*.

Who does Monteith admire as an actor? He thinks that Alec Baldwin is great, both as an actor and as an example of someone who has gone beyond just the call of acting. Monteith admires Baldwin's social conscience as an activist and the things that he does with his fame.

Monteith himself seems to be taking his fame in stride thus far. He says that the response to the show has been amazing and very "cloud nine-esque." Regarding the fact that he doesn't drink, Monteith says that he wants to "stay focused on the task at hand" and not get distracted with partying or that sort of thing. He's willing to work hard at his acting career and wants to be the best that he can be.

Though he's been working since he was a teenager, he says that he has never worked so hard in his whole life as he does on *Glee*. The actors all spend very long days filming, learning their lines, recording songs in the studio, and practicing the choreography in dance rehearsals. It's not at all unusual for the cast to spend more than a dozen hours a day devoted to working on the show. "As much as it is a lot of work," Monteith said, "we're all having the time of our lives."

Early rumors linked Monteith and fellow cast member, Lea Michele, as a potential couple in real life. However, Monteith dispelled those rumors early on. Though the two are friends and hang out on occasion when they have free time, as do many of the cast members, Monteith said, "First of all, no, we're not dating. We're like oil and water, complete opposites. I couldn't imagine what our dating life would be like. Pretty intense."

Subsequent rumors have speculated that Monteith may be dating "girl next door" country cutie celebrity Taylor Swift. The two were spotted at a Grammy pre-party together as well as out and about town at dinner. No doubt these two would make an adorable couple and would be able to relate to what it's like to be in the celebrity spotlight. Although Swift has admitted that she'd love to be a guest star on *Glee*, it appears that she and *Glee* star Monteith are likely just friends for now. Whether or not it would ever develop into anything more remains to be seen.

Regarding his love life, Monteith is constantly asked in interviews whether or not he is single. He has commented many times that the show's demanding schedule simply keeps him too busy for a real relationship at this point in his life. With his career just beginning to take off, he is certainly one of Hollywood's hottest bachelors of the moment. He did, in fact, make BuddyTV's list of "TV's 100 Sexiest Men of 2009."

When asked who his first celebrity crush was, Monteith replied that as a kid, he had a thing for the animated character She-Ra, Princess of Power, from the He-Man spin-off cartoon.

His Twitter ID, "frankenteen," is a reference from the "Acafellas" episode of *Glee*, in which the temporarily hired hard-core performance choreographer accused Finn of being freakishly tall and dragging his knuckles on the ground. Frankenteen's tweets provide some of the best behind-the-scenes happenings of the *Glee* cast. He posts everything from photos to short video clips of his fellow cast members goofing off at the Paramount studio. Monteith recently tweeted a spoiler about an upcoming guest appearance on the animated comedy television series, *The Simpsons*.

When asked in various interviews about comparisons between *Glee* and the Disney movie *High School Musical*, Monteith and show creator Ian Brennan have been known to sport the following come back: "It's like *High School Musical* has been punched in the stomach and had its lunch money stolen."

When asked what songs he'd like to perform on the

show, he said that he thinks anything by Air Supply would probably suit his character well. He'd also be interested in doing a Styx song or "I Want to Know What Love Is" by Foreigner. Though it might not suit his character Finn, he personally thinks it would be a lot of fun to do a song by Metallica. His favorite TV show theme song is the theme from *Knight Rider*.

Many of the *Glee* cast members on the show have indicated that they aren't encouraged to openly request songs for any episodes. The songs are chosen by show creator Ryan Murphy, and apparently he's likely to shoot down specific requests. However, he has been known to incorporate songs into the show that the cast happened to be singing together around the studio, just for the fun of it. The ultimate goal is to include songs that support the theme and storyline of each particular episode. Ryan Murphy's "brain is like an iPod" said Monteith, commenting on Murphy's nearly limitless knowledge of songs.

What makes *Glee* so special? According to Monteith, "The scripts are so good. You care about the characters. It's so well written, and it's so well done, and it's music that everybody's heard, you know. So, I think there's so much for so many people."

The fact that this type of

musical television series has never before been attempted is also something that makes *Glee* unique. That phenomenon also yields an unexpected result. Because this type of show has never been done before, the writers, producers, cast, and show creators are all defining a new genre as they go along. There are no previous expectations or boundaries. Therefore, according to Monteith, "It's kind of a new concept, a show like this

> "It's kind of a new concept, a show like this with this music, and so we're all figuring it out, and we're all kind of learning and growing as a group, and so there's a very collaborative kind of feel to it."

with this music, and so we're all figuring it out, and we're all kind of learning and growing as a group, and so there's a very collaborative kind of feel to it."

Monteith believes that the *Glee* characters are more than just "geek chic," but are teens and adults that people can relate to. He said, "All of us have experienced struggling with doing the right thing or doing, you know, the 'normal' thing." His character, Finn, is a stand-up guy with the courage to make good choices, not just popular decisions.

Playing the popular all-American high school jock is a bit of a stretch for Monteith, since he never experienced anything resembling a typical American high school experience. Though clearly he is a talented enough actor to sell the role whole-heartedly, acting was something that he somewhat stumbled into. Someone suggested that he should try acting, and so he enrolled in an acting class in Vancouver. It was his first acting

teacher who truly encouraged his talents and inspired him. "I was all about not going to school and partying," Monteith said. "I was rattling around and doing what was in front of me. I wasn't into acting. I didn't really have any direction."

Not just the star quarterback of the football team, Monteith's character, Finn, is the quintessential all-around athlete. True to his golden boy jock character, now that football season is over, Monteith is the captain of the basketball team in the latter portion of *Glee* Season One.

JAYMA MAYS

as Emma Pillsbury

Jayma Mays portrays McKinley High's plucky, germaphobic guidance counselor, Emma Pillsbury, who harbors a not-so-secret crush on Glee Club instructor, Will Schuester. Commenting on whether she was anything like her character in real life, Mays said, "I'm not, thank goodness. Although I have to say it, after the first few weeks, after we got picked up and we started filming the first few episodes,

I kind of started getting that feeling of needing to wash my hands all the time. And I started keeping anti-bacterial stuff in my purse, just because you start thinking about that stuff more, just naturally, because they're kind of shoving it in your face at work all the time. I'm not wearing rubber gloves at home, but I definitely keep a little Purell in my pocketbook now."

Jamia Suzette Mays grew up in Virginia, where she attended Grundy Senior High School in Grundy, VA. She attended college in Virginia, first at Southwest Virginia Community College where she earned an associate's degree and performed in their theatre program. She spent the next year at Virginia Tech in Blacksburg, and later she continued on to Radford University where she earned a degree in performing arts.

Named after her father, James Mays, she eventually changed her name from Jemia to Jayma along the way. She was a natural entertainer, and she idolized Lucille Ball and Carol Burnett, two red-headed actresses with a talent for comedy. As a child, Mays could often be found spending time at home singing and dancing, playing the piano, reciting lines from *Annie*, and asking her mother to make costumes for her. She entertained her family, her parents' friends, her teachers, and almost any audience that happened to be near her.

When her local community theater decided to put on a production of *Annie*, Mays was quick to audition. However, she wasn't awarded a part, and her parents reported that she was absolutely crushed. However, she persevered and continued to do the things that she loved, though at the time, she had no inkling that she would some day be a famous actress. "I really didn't think acting was an option for me," Mays said. "You just don't think

SAY ANYTHING . . .

Jayma Mays plays McKinley High's caring guidance counselor, Emma Pillsbury, with understated subtlety. No matter how ridiculous the situation, her lines never come across as too over-the-top because Mays' soft-spoken delivery makes them slip by, leaving viewers with an almost hit-and-run comedic punch line. Here are a few favorites:

"I have trouble with things like that, the messy things."
(From the pilot episode.)

"Okay, but I still want to talk about the feelings that you had that led up to you wanting to puke your guts out."
(From the "Showmance" episode.)

"A few years ago, I started an online flirtation with a high school fling, Andy. Things got weird, and I called it off, and two months later, Versace was dead."
(From "The Rhodes Not Taken" episode.)

"Kurt, I'm a girl who knows her solvents, and your breath smells like rubbing alcohol."
(From "The Rhodes Not Taken" episode.)

"We've got a problem. They're doing all of our numbers. The kids are completely freaking out. Artie keeps ramming himself into the wall, and I'm pretty sure that Jacob Israel just wet himself." (From the "Sectionals" episode.)

"He understood that I wasn't doing it for the kids. I was doing it for you." (To Will in the "Sectionals" episode.)

that, growing up."

What was Mays like in high school? "I don't think I necessarily fit into one particular group and to one clique," Mays said. "I did the cheerleader thing, I was a cheerleader, so I was a part of that group. But also, I was a total nerd. I loved math, and I would do the little math competitions that we had at school. And we didn't have a drama department, but we had this small group where you'd go and compete doing monologues and stuff so I was also in that group. So, I did a ton of different stuff, which really didn't make me feel like I was a part of one particular group, but sort of a part of many."

Mays stood out in her small Virginia town where the main industry was coal mining. "I definitely know that I'm quirky. I know that I'm different," Mays said. "Red hair definitely made me different growing up."

With a teacher mentor much along the lines of Mr. Schuester, Mays' high school teacher, Debbie Raines, encouraged her to follow her dreams. Raines introduced Mays to the art of drama and public speaking. Mays

Photo: Amy Sussman/Getty Images

JAYMA MAYS AND MATTHEW MORRISON

Glee is not the first time that Jayma Mays and Matthew Morrison have crossed paths. Before they played Emma and Will, they worked together on the television comedy pilot, *Nice Girls Don't Get the Corner Office*. Mays starred in the show as Angela, the sweet career girl trying to get ahead in the corporate man's world. Morrison played Brody, Angela's friend, who sported tattoos and sang in an under-appreciated rock band.

referred to it as her "first real introduction to doing acting and doing drama and doing stuff in front of people. It's not just me being at home and entertaining the family but actually doing something with that skill." Raines encouraged Mays to reach for something bigger. "She kind of pushed me into thinking, 'You can do this. This is something you should consider, and don't

give up on this idea.'"

Eventually moving to Los Angeles to pursue her dream, Mays enjoyed a successful acting career, both in television and on the silver screen, prior to starting work on *Glee*. She seems to have built a career on playing quirky love interests.

She made her television debut in a guest role on the *Friends* spin-off series, *Joey*. She played a character named Molly, who turned out to be the fake girlfriend of a college boy trying to impress his friend.

One of her most memorable roles was in the television hit

"Poor Matt. I stepped on Matt's feet about a thousand times that day [when we were] dancing."

series, *Heroes*, where she played Charlie Andrews, the true love of main character Hiro Nakamura, played by Masi Oka. In this recurring role that spanned multiple seasons, Mays portrayed Charlie as a sweet small town waitress with the special ability of having a photographic memory. She is able to absorb and learn anything she sees, reads, or hears.

Mays met her husband, actor Adam Campbell, while they were both starring in the humorous parody film *Epic Movie*. Mays played a character named Lucy, and Campbell played Peter in this comedy that spoofed other films and characters. She also co-starred as the love interest In the movie *Paul Blart: Mall Cop*, with Kevin James.

Though she has played both comedic and dramatic roles, none of her previous acting credits prior to *Glee* included singing and dancing. When she performed in the number "I Could Have Danced All Night," Mays was really quite anxious about it. "I actually found that terrifying," Mays said. "I haven't had to do that before on camera, and I was so nervous that day. I had to keep eating bread and toast because my stomach was so sick. But it was an interesting experience. It was definitely a challenge for me. Of course if they ask me to do it again, I

would do it again, but I'm not going to go begging them for it. Poor Matt. I stepped on Matt's feet about a thousand times that day [when we were] dancing."

Commenting on Emma's adversarial relationship with Terri Schuester who is played by Jessalyn Gilsig, Mays said,

Photo by: Trae Patton/NBCU Photo Bank via AP Images

Jayma Mays as Charlie Andrews, the ill-fated waitress and girlfriend of Hiro Nakamura (Masi Oka) in *Heroes*.

"We are actually really close. [Referring to Gilsig.] And it is funny...I think I'm probably closer with her than anyone else on set. So, the fact that we are like arch-enemies [on the show], it's really strange. But I actually think that makes it more fun, because it is totally a

make believe scenario that we kind of play with when we have scenes together."

When asked about her character, Mays is thoughtful, "She is a romantic at heart, but she's practical. She's got this very dreamy side about her and who she wants to be and what she wants her life to be like. But she's also got this very practical, down-to-earth, 'well this is kind of the best I can do' thing.

"It's funny, people think that part of her is weak, but I don't think that's true. It's her being practical. People are like that sometimes."

KEVIN McHALE
as Artie Abrams

Kevin McHale plays Artie Abrams, the McKinley High Glee Club guitar player in a wheelchair. Artie wears glasses and has a sweet demeanor. He is well-liked by fellow Glee Clubbers, but is sometimes the target of school bullies. For his show audition, McHale sang the Beatles song "Let It Be." Claiming in an interview that he didn't even know all the words to the song, combined with the fact that there was a roomful

of people outside who were also waiting to audition, made that first audition experience a little nerve-wracking. Though he was just as anxious during his second call-back, he used that nervous energy to portray the character. "I think the nervousness helped," said McHale, "because I intentionally kind of pushed that into Artie."

Glee choreographer, Zach Woodlee, speculated that McHale is probably the best dancer in the Glee cast, but since his character is confined to a wheelchair,

they've had to figure out some alternative ways for McHale to strut his stuff. The actor has become pretty adept at dancing on the show, even in a wheelchair. In the "Wheels" episode of Glee, the entire cast followed his lead and took to wheelchairs to perform the song "Proud Mary."

Commenting on what it's like to play Artie, particularly the aspect about him being a character in a wheelchair, McHale said, "It's just part of the character. As an actor, you want something that kind

of challenges you, and that was just natural. As soon as I get in that kind of wardrobe, with suspenders and a belt, I just kind of get into that." He did admit that it was difficult to stop tapping his feet to the beat of the songs in the beginning, since he wasn't consciously aware that he was doing it in the first place.

McHale prepared for the role by reaching out to some friends and acquaintances in wheelchairs, including an old high school teacher, to talk to them about their experiences and to try to get a feel for how to play the part realistically. While on tour, McHale received a lot of positive feedback from fans in wheelchairs who could indentify with and relate to his character.

What was Kevin McHale like in high school? McHale describes himself as someone who "kind of went between the different cliques" in high school and "didn't really have one place where [he] belonged." He said that was "by design," not really wanting to get type-cast into a particular group. He was into music and acting, but he didn't participate in any school clubs or extracurricular activities.

McHale doesn't play guitar in real life as well as they portray on the show. He's sort of had to learn as he goes along, in order to make the

SAY ANYTHING . . .

McHale's character, Artie, is a likable nerd who knows who he is and is proud to express it through music. Here are a few of Artie's great lines from the show:

"We're planning on smacking them down like the hand of God." (From the "Vitamin D" episode.)

"I hope we don't get in trouble for our covert jam session." (From the "Throwdown" episode.)

"You've never been hit by a slushy before, Mr. Schu?" (From the "Mash-Up" episode.)

"Well, you're irritating most of the time, but don't take that personally." (To Rachel in the "Wheels" episode.)

"Dudes, this is serious. If she finds out, she's going to tell Finn. She's a total trout mouth." (Talking about Rachel in the "Sectionals" episode.)

"Perhaps I could improvise some of my def poetry jams." (From the "Sectionals" episode.)

> **"I think 90% of the people in high school don't fit in with the popular kids. So we're touching on something that most people can relate to."**

Photo: S.Bergman/JPegFoto/PictureGroup via AP IMAGES

numbers in the show seem authentic.

Who was McHale's favorite singer growing up? "Michael Jackson, hands down, from an early age," McHale said. "From the age of three, I was aware of Michael Jackson. Like when I was little, people would ask me my name, and I would either say 'Mickey Mouse' or 'Michael Jackson.'" He admitted to asking his mother to buy him Michael Jackson shoes and to having nightmares about the "Thriller" video.

Matthew Morrison was not the only *Glee* cast member to star in a boy band. Kevin McHale performed in the boy band NLT, which stands for "Not Like Them." Their harmonizing pop songs had a bit of an R&B influence. Some of their songs included "She Said, I Said," "That Girl," and "Karma." They also had a song on the 2007 *Bratz* movie

soundtrack titled "Heartburn."

McHale made the transition from music to acting fairly seamlessly. He appeared on an episode of the hit comedy series *The Office*, and he was also in multiple episodes of *Zoey 101*, where he played the recurring role of Dooley.

McHale appeared in multiple episodes of *True Blood,* an HBO series based on the Southern Vampire novels by Charlaine Harris. His character, Neil Jones, was the coroner's assistant and a

fangbanger (a human who is a vampire groupie) who died when he was burned in a fire. McHale said that he wasn't really into vampires and didn't know much about *True Blood* when he auditioned, since it hadn't started airing yet. He only had to read a few words for his audition. Commenting on his *True Blood* experience, he said, "It was fun, but I wish I didn't get killed off so quickly."

McHale has a fondness for bowties and suspenders. In an interview, he once commented, "Not just Bill Nye can rock a bowtie."

In their free time between takes, McHale said that the cast sometimes play a role-playing game called *Mafia*. They celebrated his June 14, 2009, birthday with a *Mafia* theme, and cast members, writers, and production assistants alike all played together.

Keeping friends and fans up to date via Twitter, McHale posts as "druidDUDE." He tweets about music, some of the things he does with his free time, and of course *Glee*.

McHale enjoys going on tour and meeting fans, hearing their stories, and finding out why they connect so much with the show. When asked in an interview for PopEater why a show about unpopular kids is so popular, McHale responded, "If we've learned anything by having all these signings and everything, it's that people come up to us, and it's probably the coolest part of the job, and say like 'Thank you for playing us on TV—the outcasts, the weirdos, the losers.' But I think 90% of the people in high school don't fit in with the popular kids. So we're touching on something that most people can relate to.

"I think what's realistic about the show is that, at some point, each of our characters is put into a situation or something that breaks the stereotype."

McHale said that one of his favorite things about being a cast member of *Glee* is getting to do scenes with Jane Lynch who plays Sue Sylvester. He also really enjoys working with the later additions to the New Directions Glee Club choir: Heather Morris who plays the ditsy blond cheerleader Brittany, Naya Rivera who plays cheerleader Santana Lopez, Harry Shum who plays Mike Chang, and Dijon Talton who plays Matt Rutherford. He said that Morris and Rivera are "probably my favorites to watch."

According to McHale, the music from the show helps attract fans and gives people from all different backgrounds and age groups a powerful connection. He loves that the songs are drawn from different genres—show tunes, rock, pop—and they get to interpret them in different ways to fit a story and serve the overall theme.

He thinks this is what makes *Glee* unique and enjoyable for the actors and for the audience. "It's this whole new kind of experiment that we're all a part of. The show has no boundaries, no rules. We're beyond happy with how it's going so far."

AP Photo/Chris Pizzello

CHRIS COLFER

as Kurt Hummel

Chris Colfer plays the role of Kurt Hummel, a character not originally included in the initial concept of the show, but who has become the super breakout star of the series. A fashionable and confident gay male soprano with a flair for the dramatic, the character of Kurt and the skilled way in which Colfer portrays him has fans cheering for more. Chris Colfer auditioned for *Glee* with no previous professional acting experience

shortly after graduating from high school. His father drove him to the audition. Originally trying for the role of Artie Abrams, casting director Robert Ulrich decided he wasn't the right fit for that particular character, but he was so well liked that they invited him back and created the Kurt Hummel role specifically for him.

While adding the role of Kurt Hummel, another character got cut from the script. Originally, a character named Rajish was to be a member of the McKinley High Glee Club, but once Murphy met Colfer, Rajish was out and Kurt was in.

For his audition, Colfer sang the song "Mr. Cellophane" from *Chicago*. He had practiced the song at home with his grandmother before the audition. The song was later written into the pilot episode of the show for him to sing for his Glee Club audition for Mr. Schu.

Colfer said that he was always nervous in auditions, but that his *Glee* audition was extra nerve-wracking because he was expected to sing in front of Ryan Murphy, an entertainment industry icon whom Colfer idolized. When they met, Ryan Murphy asked Colfer if he'd been in *The Sound of Music*, and Colfer quipped back, "I know, I have Von Trapp written all over me." Colfer told Murphy that he had played the character Kurt in *The Sound of Music*, which ultimately led to the decision to name his new character "Kurt" as well. The character's last name, "Hummel," is a result of the casting executives deciding that Colfer reminded them of a small Hummel ceramic figurine "with rosy cheeks," like those who Murphy's own mother collected when he was growing up.

The role of Kurt is somewhat autobiographically-based on things that happened in Murphy's own life. Colfer was completely blown away that Murphy actually created a character for him in order to incorporate him into the show. "Everything that's happened I can understand except for that part," Colfer said. "That part is completely mind-blowing. Every time I think of it my eyes get wide and I just can't believe it. It means the world to me because I want to do what Ryan does someday."

When Colfer first learned that his character would be gay, the thought initially made him quite anxious. "At first, I was absolutely terrified because I'm from a very conservative anti-gay town," Colfer said. However, he quickly came to terms with his character's identity and embraced it, portraying Kurt as not just proud but with a sense of outright superiority.

The storyline written for his character has been delivered with sensitivity, a healthy dose of humor, and respect. This is particularly true in the episode where Kurt came out to his father. The uniquely ground-breaking thing about the character of Kurt is that, though he struggles and is sometimes made fun of for being gay, ultimately, he has good friends, a decent father, and a supportive network of people who accept him. Being gay is just one aspect of who the character is, but there's so much more.

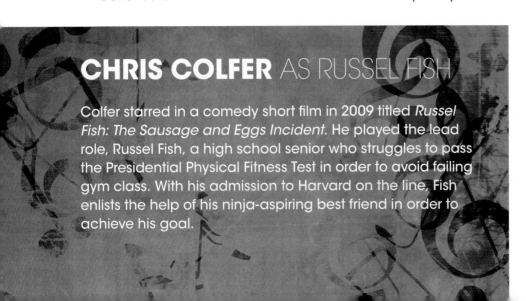

CHRIS COLFER AS RUSSEL FISH

Colfer starred in a comedy short film in 2009 titled *Russel Fish: The Sausage and Eggs Incident*. He played the lead role, Russel Fish, a high school senior who struggles to pass the Presidential Physical Fitness Test in order to avoid failing gym class. With his admission to Harvard on the line, Fish enlists the help of his ninja-aspiring best friend in order to achieve his goal.

"I was made fun of a lot in high school because of the way I sound and the way I was. I was a lone duck in a swan-filled pond."

CHRIS COLFER AS KURT HUMMEL

Not only did he inspire the character, but Colfer has also served as the motivation for some of the story lines as well. As a student, he begged to sing the song "Defying Gravity" from *Wicked* for the school talent show, but he wasn't allowed to because it was considered a female song. After telling Murphy of his experience in casual conversation one day, Murphy wrote a similar incident into the "Wheels" episode of *Glee*.

Born in the small farming town of Clovis, CA, Colfer said he knew that he wanted to be an actor "since I was an embryo." He attended Clovis East High School, where he won speech and debate awards and participated in theater. During school, Colfer wrote, directed and starred in a *Sweeney Todd*–inspired musical spoof titled *Shirley Todd*. The play was performed as a "Senior Showcase" for his graduating class, and it was set in modern day England with punk rock–style characters.

As a teen, Colfer was in a community theater production of Disney's *Beauty and the Beast*, in which he played the young teacup, Chip. He designed his own costume for the role, and his parents helped him make it.

Colfer claims that he "can completely relate to the characters on *Glee*," particularly because he felt that he was "a complete underdog in high school." He was very active in performing arts in high school, and he was also the president and the only member of his school's Writer's Club. As his float for the Homecoming parade, he

SAY ANYTHING . . .

Colfer's character, Kurt Hummel, is known for his fashion sense and snappy commentary. Almost all of his lines are memorable, but here are a few of the best:

"Please, this is Marc Jacobs' new collection."
(Before being thrown into the dumpster by the football team.)

"They're going to throw fruit at us, and I just had a facial."
(From the "Showmance" episode.)

"It's a unitard. Guys wear them to work out nowadays, do sports. They lick sweat from the body... All the guys in football wear them. They're jock-chic."
(From the "Preggers" episode.)

"She'd massacre Mariah in a diva-off."
(From "The Rhodes Not Taken" episode.)

"They declined my offer to do their hair in cornrows, and all of my artistic decisions have been derided as too costly because they involve several varieties of exotic bird feathers."
(From the "Vitamin D" episode.)

"We all know I'm more popular than Rachel, and I dress better than her, but I want you to promise me that you're going to vote for whoever sings the song better."
(From the "Wheels" episode.)

"I don't know why I find his stupidity charming. I mean, he's cheating off a girl who thinks the square root of four is 'rainbows.' I guess that's love for you."
(From the "Ballad" episode.)

"Damn her talent."
(Talking about Rachel in the "Sectionals" episode.)

CHRIS COLFER AS KURT HUMMEL

displayed a large poster in a pick-up truck that read "Join Writer's Club. It's the 'write' decision."

Colfer said that he didn't have many friends in high school. He worked in the cafeteria before school, spent much of his free time writing and participating in community theater, and devoted time to his younger sister, Hannah, who has been in and out of the hospital many times throughout her young life due to an illness that she's had since birth. Colfer knew what he wanted and knew who he was, but he was always different from other kids in school, and it made him stick out. "I was made fun of a lot in high school because of the way I sound and the way I was," Colfer said. "I was a lone duck in a swan-filled pond."

Describing the characters in *Glee*, Colfer says that "They just want to be a part of something. They're just kind of lost souls wandering the halls, and they just want to have the feeling that they belong." It sounds like this is something that Colfer himself could relate to, as do the many gleek fans who tune in to watch the show each week.

Colfer spent much of his youth performing, up to four nights a week, in community theater programs. His parents were very supportive, always willing to drive him to rehearsals and auditions, while encouraging his love for acting. At the age of eight, Colfer played the Charles Schultz character of Snoopy in his first play. His mother, Karyn Colfer, recalled, "I saw a light go on in my son that has never turned off."

His parents knew that their son had something special to offer, and they fostered his creativity out of sheer love. They simply wanted to see him happy. "We had this child, Christopher, who was extremely gifted in all areas," Karyn Colfer said. "He was very smart academically. He was very mature for his age because of his sister's illness. And this was his outlet. It was a way for him to have something that was his very own, and his father and I committed to making sure that he went after this."

While still in high school, he secured an agent in Los Angeles, who happened to be "a family friend of a friend." He and his parents made the long drive from

During an interview performed in front of fans in Los Angeles, *Glee* cast members unanimously agreed that Colfer was the funniest individual amongst them.

CHRIS COLFER AS KURT HUMMEL

Clovis to L.A., which took about four hours each direction, for many auditions while he was still in high school. His big break came shortly after high school when he was chosen as a member of the *Glee* cast, and it seems evident that Colfer is here to stay.

Commenting on why *Glee* appeals to high school kids so much, Colfer claims that, "The show has struck a chord with an audience that never had anything to relate to before. I know personally, because I am that audience, I'm one of those kids."

Though he says that he doesn't possess any of Kurt's natural fashion sense himself, Colfer says that he loves Kurt's wardrobe. It's very different from how he normally dresses, admitting that he's "more of a jeans and T-shirt boy." It seems to be great fun wearing those couture garments that are seen on the runway during Fashion Week in New York, though he says that the super tight skinny jeans aren't always the most comfortable option. He was particularly impressed by the full length transparent Dolce & Gabbana raincoat with sailor suit style cuffs on the wrist. He jokingly speculated that Kurt's high-end designer wardrobe is probably about half of the show's budget.

Playing the role of Kurt is not all wardrobe changes and snappy remarks. The singing skills required to play Kurt are highly specialized. In the "Wheels" episode of *Glee*, Kurt had to hit a high F note in the song "Defying Gravity." This is no easy task for a female soprano, and there are few men who could say they've done it, much less in front of cameras while being filmed for a major network television show.

During an interview performed in front of fans in Los Angeles, *Glee* cast members unanimously agreed that Colfer was the funniest individual amongst them.

a few words for myself."

"Every time I get injured I measure its severity by asking myself 'Would this stop me from going to Disneyland?'"

"My Twitter account has been verified!!! This must be what Pinocchio felt like when he became a real boy!"

"A red carpet and press line at a funeral has to be the tackiest thing in the world and I want one at mine someday."

"I've never found anything I can't do after lots of practice and focus...except algebra 2."

"I never thought I'd be a member of the Grammys!!! Then again, I never thought

> **Born in the small farming town of Clovis, CA, Colfer said he knew that he wanted to be an actor "since I was an embryo."**

He keeps family, friends, and fans up-to-date with regular tweets, Colfer is as witty on Twitter as he is an actor. Here's a sample of some of his hilarious one-liner social news feed updates:

"I tried reenacting Pink's Grammy performance with a blanket and duct tape. Epic fail."

"I keep hearing about all these 'Chris Colfer' sightings at different places. If I ever run into me I'm going to have

I'd be in the Future Farmers of America in high school either."

When asked what song he'd like to perform on *Glee*, he said that he thinks it would be great fun to have the cast perform "Time Warp" from *The Rocky Horror Picture Show*. Commenting on his character's depth and story lines, Colfer said, "He definitely opens up that Pandora's box of emotions and goes for it."

MARK SALLING

as Puck

Mark Salling plays the role of Noah Puckerman, better known as Puck, the McKinley High football star and bully who feels he has a solid enough reputation as a stud that being in Glee Club won't hurt his popularity in the least. Puck is also the real father of Quinn's baby. Though the name Puck is short for the character's last name, Puckerman, it may also serve as a reference to the mythological sprite character,

A biting comedy for the unc

the mischievous Robin Goodfellow also known as Puck, from Shakespeare's *A Midsummer's Night Dream*.

The mohawk hairstyle worn by his character was inspired by Stalling himself. For his audition, he cut his hair into a mohawk in order to stand out. It was a bit of a risk, but one that paid off. The casting directors not only remembered him, but the show creators incorporated the trademark hairstyle into the role.

Despite the fact that Salling clearly made an impression during his audition, he was not automatically given the part right away. He returned for five separate auditions, eventually beating out some other well known actors before being cast in the role of Puck.

He jokingly told *Good Day LA* that when he auditioned for *Glee*, he had about $300 left in his savings account and was considering moving back in with his parents in Texas if his career didn't catch a break soon. Fortunately for Puck fans, Salling stayed in Los Angeles and became everyone's favorite gleeky bad boy.

Salling says that his life hasn't changed a whole lot since the success of *Glee*. He told talk show host Wendy Williams, "You go home and you see your friends, and they're very quick to make sure that you don't get a big head." While he's still close with his old friends, he also describes his fellow *Glee* cast members as "family" and "all best friends," claiming he likes everyone. He wasn't prepared for the show's resounding success, but said that in the beginning, he was just eager for the opportunity to work with show creator Ryan Murphy.

Referring to his new-found success, Salling said that one of the coolest things was just watching an episode of the show with his grandmother. As the actor who portrays the show's sexy bad boy character, it is no surprise that he is frequently asked in interviews whether or not he is single. He once replied, "My Mom and Grandma are the number one women in my life," but he added with a sly look and a knowing nod to the camera that "there may also be someone special."

Salling's real life interests are not all football and Glee Club. Growing up in Dallas, TX, he was on the wrestling team for a while but didn't play football, and music was the primary creative outlet on which he focused his energies

SAY ANYTHING . . .

Mark Salling plays the character Noah "Puck" Puckerman, who is both a rebel and a jock. Here are a few favorite Puck lines:

"I've got star potential, and more specifically, I'm tired of wasting my time with high school girls... See, young girls will shoot you down and make you feel terrible about yourself, but a cougar never disappoints." (From the "Acafellas" episode.)

"I'm a stud, dude. I could wear a dress to school, and people would think it's cool." (From the "Preggers" episode.)

"The wheelchair kid's right. That Rachel chick makes me want to light myself on fire, but she can sing." (From "The Rhodes Not Taken" episode.)

"Are you questioning my bad-assness? Have you seen my guns?" (Referring to his biceps in the "Mash-Up" episode.)

"Does this have to happen tonight? Because I have my fight club." (From the "Sectionals" episode.)

in high school. He said he was "a bit of a hippie" and "pretty mellow" as a teen. He got along with everyone and was comfortable making friends with people from all different groups. He plays the piano, guitar, bass, and drums, and he performed in a rock band throughout high school.

"My Mom and Grandma are the number one women in my life."

Beginning his acting career at a very young age, Salling's first film role was in the 1996 horror movie *Children of the Corn: The Gathering*. In this fourth installment of the *Children of the Corn* films, Salling played the character James Rhodes in this direct-to-DVD movie.

Salling also played in another horror film, *The Grave-* *yard*. In this slasher movie, his character, Eric, was short-lived (literally); he was the first member of a group of friends to die a bloody death while goofing off in a cemetery.

In another TV appearance prior to *Glee*, Salling had a guest role in an episode of *Walker, Texas Ranger*. The episode titled "Rise to the Occasion" was set in a school and featured kids who were bullied by gang members.

A talented musician, Salling writes his own music. For his latest band, Jericho, Salling wrote and sang the lyrics as well as produced the songs for the tracks on his "Smoke Signals" CD. The songs on "Smoke Signals" are an

alternative version of an indie rock sound, but Salling likes to explore all genres of music.

In real life, Salling is more charitable than his character counterpart, Puck. He volunteers his time to help the James Hunter Wildlife Rescue charity. After the devastating earthquake in Haiti, he pledged 10 percent of his merchandise product sales from his website, marksalling-music.com, towards the Red Cross' disaster relief efforts in Haiti.

Several self-produced music videos featuring his original music can be seen on his marksallingmusic.com website. In addition to being able to listen to and purchase his music on the site, he also offers merchandise for sale, including T-shirts and autographed posters. Salling's band is expected to go on tour in the summer of 2010.

Salling says he will always work on his music because it's something that he truly loves and it's a part of him. "I'm always writing and performing," he told JustJared.com. However, he's not sure how much of a focus it will be during his time with *Glee*. Not only does the show take up much of his time, but Salling joked of his FOX network contract, "It's just a matter of what Uncle Fox and Aunt Sony are going to allow me to do."

Salling is more polite than

MARK SALLING AS PUCK

his character, Puck. The manners that he was raised with still come through in his everyday personality. In several interviews, he referred to talk show hosts as "sir" or "ma'am," sometimes taking them aback with his Texan niceties.

In the "Mash-Up" episode of *Glee*, Salling performed the Neil Diamond song "Sweet Caroline," which he said was satisfying because Neil Diamond is his mom's favorite artist. His character, Puck, sang the song in an effort to woo fellow Glee Clubber, Rachel, played by Lea Michele.

Will we see more sparks between Puck and Rachel? "We never expected that to catch on quite so well," said *Glee* creator Brad Falchuk regarding the brief hook-up between Puck and Rachel. "So we'll have to do something about that." There are fan websites and discussion boards dedicated to the two as a potential couple, though to be fair, there are also sites devoted to the followers in the Rachel and Finn camp as well. Who will Rachel end up with? Guess we'll just have to watch and see.

When asked what possible songs might be on his wish list to sing on *Glee* some day, Salling replied that he'd like to do a Radiohead song or something by Nine Inch Nails for a different change of pace. Ultimately though, he'd love to do an original song at some point. As a songwriter and music composer himself, he'd probably no doubt love to do something that he wrote.

What does Salling think makes *Glee* so special? "You can't watch it and not smile and not want to see it again," said Salling. "I dare you to try."

AP Photo/Vince Bucci

AMBER RILEY

as Mercedes Jones

Amber Riley plays the soulful and sassy Glee Club diva, Mercedes Jones, who stands up for what she believes and isn't afraid to tell you about it. For her *Glee* audition, Amber Riley sang the song "Sweet Thing," but she was put on the spot spur-of-the-moment and asked to sing "And I'm Telling You," a song from *Dream Girls*. While Riley was extremely nervous to perform a song that she had never sung before, *Glee* casting

A biting comedy for the underdog in all of us.

Photo by Alberto E. Rodriguez/Getty Images

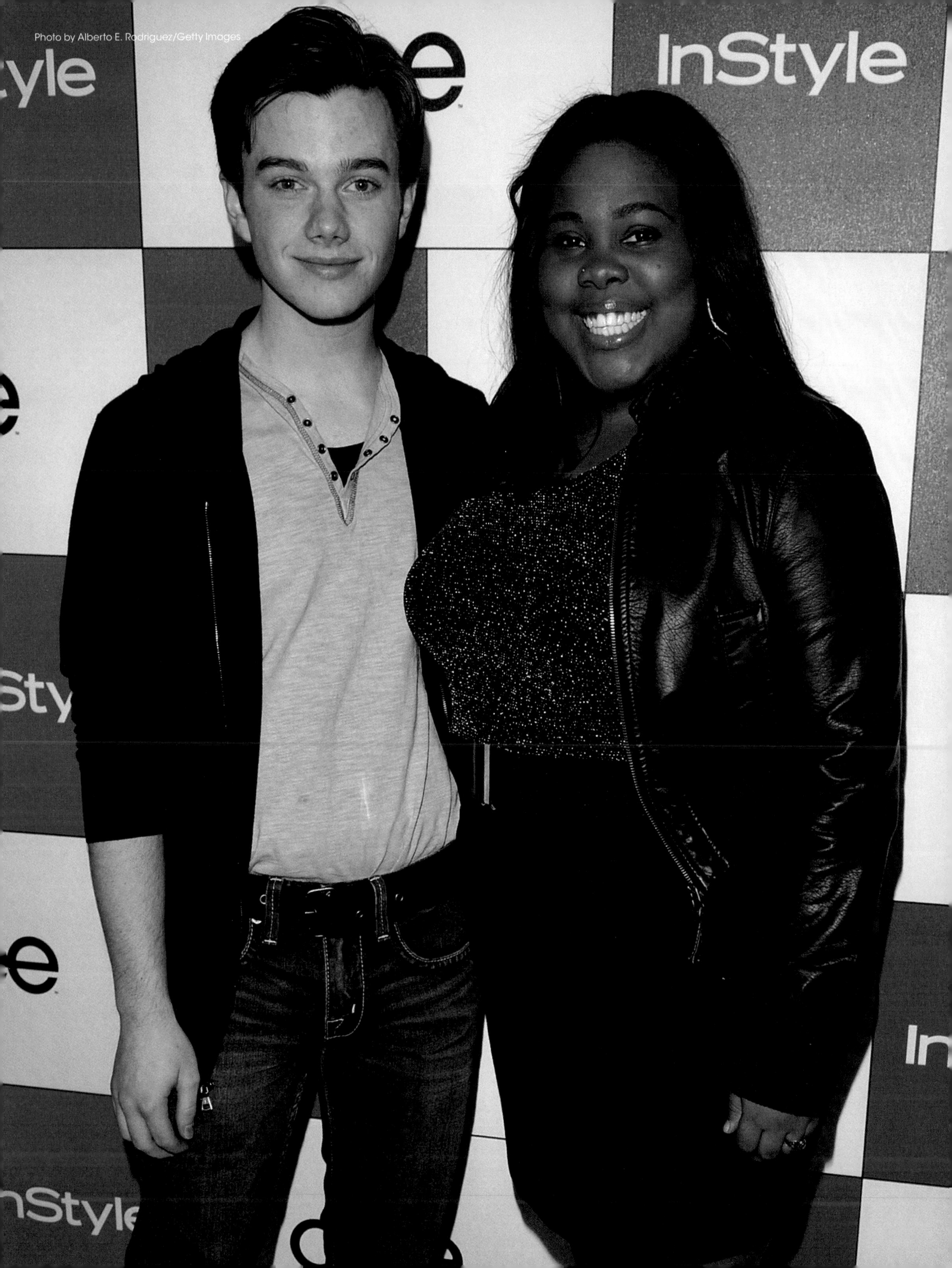

director Robert Ulrich claimed that just two lines into the song, he knew that he had found the right actress to play Mercedes.

"I heard about *Glee* at the end of the audition process," said Riley. "I went in initially thinking the role was more of a background gig and soon learned it was a co-starring role! Everything happened so fast, and I'm blessed to be a part of something so influential to young people and to be having so much fun living a part of my dream."

Glee was not the first time that Riley and show creator Ryan Murphy had crossed paths. While Riley was still a teen, she was cast in a television pilot for another show written by Murphy titled *St. Sass*. Unfortunately, the show was not picked up to become a series. Commenting on Murphy's instrumental role in her career, Riley said, "I guess you could say he gave me my start, and now he's given me my second start." After the *St. Sass* pilot, Riley joined the ensemble cast in the sketch comedy television series *Cedric the Entertainer*.

About her character on the show, Riley said, "Mercedes Jones is a self-proclaimed diva, I believe, in the Glee Club. She brings a lot of truth. She brings a lot of drama. She brings a lot of fun to the Glee Club, but a lot of attitude, a whole lot of attitude."

Actor Chris Colfer who plays Kurt said that his favorite *Glee* songs are "anything that Amber does" adding that "she blows everything out of the water." Colfer and Riley are good friends and are sometimes spotted shopping together or hanging out off the set. They've both talked in interviews about how they love to shop at Target. Colfer is more than just her friend and co-star. Riley said, "My role model for acting is Chris Colfer."

"I've been singing since I was two-years-old," Riley said. "I have a musical family." In an effort to nurture her interest in music, Riley's mother encouraged her along the way, enrolling her in a wide variety of vocal lessons, including jazz, gospel, and Italian aria. She claims to have what she jokingly refers to as "a singer's Tourette's [Syndrome]." She breaks out into song whenever and wherever the mood strikes her. Though the formula for the show isn't to suddenly burst out into song, if anyone could pull off a scene like that, it would be Riley. Music seems to be running through her veins.

SAY ANYTHING . . .

Amber Riley plays the chic and sassy Glee Club diva, Mercedes Jones. She is confident, brutally honest, and not afraid to tell it like it is. Here are a few of the greatest lines from Mercedes:

"Come on, we can do this in our sleep. You think those six dudes are going to give us any competition? I say we just wing it." (From the "Vitamin D" episode.)

"Don't make me take you to the carpet." (From the "Throwdown" episode.)

"If Finn and Quinn got nailed, none of us are safe." (From the "Mash-Up" episode.)

"As soon as I get my record deal, I'm not speaking to any of you." (From the "Mattress" episode.)

"Okay, you know what Miss Bossy Pants, enough. I've worked just as hard as you, and I'm just as good as you. You know, you always end up stealing the spotlight." (To Rachel in the "Sectionals" episode.)

Riley grew up in southern California, where she attended La Mirada High School. Her family now lives in Long Beach, CA. Commenting on her high school experience, Riley said, "I kind of had a life outside of high school. I was singing in background, singing in choir, studio work. There wasn't a Glee Club in my school, and if there was, I sincerely apologize, I had no idea." In another interview, she elaborated, "I didn't really have a bad high school experience. I think I had like a normal high school experience. I kind of hung out with everyone. I was a drama nerd. I don't like to think that we were nerds. I just like to think that we were intelligent. But I mean, you know, my high school experience really wasn't that bad."

Riley has a background in theater and has performed with the Los Angeles Opera. She played parts in *A Midsummer Night's Dream*, *Alice in Wonderland*, *Mystery on the Docks*, and *Into the Woods*.

Before joining the cast of *Glee*, Riley once auditioned for another musical FOX television series, *American Idol*. She was just 17-years-old at the time, and though she made it past the first round of auditions, she did not make the final cut for the show. About the experience, Riley said, "It

kind of humbled me a lot and made me work harder." In another interview, she stated that, at the time it happened, she felt like her "world was over." However, she bounced back and persevered, continuing to do what she loved best, and that was sing. She said, "It gave me a chance to work on my craft, to work on my voice, to work on my confidence." It seems to have worked out for the best because fans certainly adore

her as Mercedes.

Riley keeps her friends and fans up to date with frequent Twitter updates as "MsAmberRiley." She tweets about a wide range of topics, including how she spends her time, the television shows she watches, and her strong faith in God. Here's a sample of a few of her Twitter social feed updates:

"Listening to Amy Winehouse *Back to Black* album. Classic. Exactly the kind of

Photo by Lisa Lake/Getty Images

album I wanna cut."

"Happy Valentines Day! Take this opportunity to let those u love know how u feel. And know God loves u if u feel no one else does!"

"Hey guys! I'm being Simpsonized!!!! This will probably be my most memorable moment of the year! Aaaah!"

Commenting on her character, Riley said, "Mercedes Jones is a diva. She likes to wear nice clothes, and she likes to tell people that she's wearing nice clothes, and she always wears gold hoops [earrings]. She's a really fun character to play. There are some bold clothes that I wear that I would never attempt to wear ever [in real life]. I like the fact that she's confident, and that she gives a good example to other young girls. I really like my character. She's very, very confident."

What is Riley's own fashion style? "I like to describe my style as comfortable classy chic," said Riley. "I love to have clothes that I can mix and match to either dress up or dress down. I have expensive pieces in my closet, but this girl does not turn a blind eye to the sales rack. I

"Everything happened so fast, and I'm blessed to be a part of something so influential to young people and to be having so much fun living a part of my dream."

love a bargain! Fashion knows no price tag in my eyes. I believe Mercedes and I share the same love of color. I love being bright and vibrant and colorful. I like to say I'm Mercedes all grown up. She's more hip hop than me, for sure."

Riley told talk show host Bonnie Hunt that she "models her life after Mercedes." She expanded on the topic by explaining that they're both real divas. She admires the confidence and self-assurance that her character has at such a young age, and they both seem to have the courage to go after what they want.

Like her fellow cast member, Mark Salling, who plays Puck, Riley also writes her own songs. If she had her choice of any song, she would love to perform one of her own original songs for the show some day.

What does Riley think about *Glee* and what makes the show so appealing? "We have a really good chemistry off screen, so it shows a lot on screen. I also think people love the diversity. They love the honesty of the show, the transparency of the show. It deals with so many different issues, but comes at it at a realistic angle. Our writers are so amazing. They take cues from us and listen to us, being that we haven't been out of high school that long."

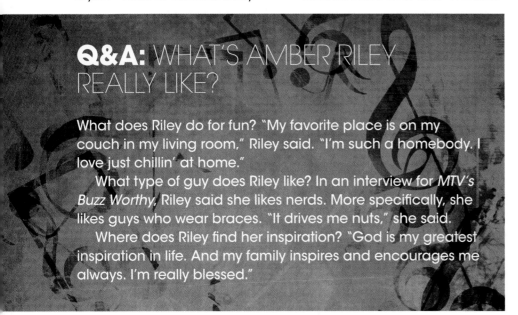

Q&A: WHAT'S AMBER RILEY REALLY LIKE?

What does Riley do for fun? "My favorite place is on my couch in my living room," Riley said. "I'm such a homebody. I love just chillin' at home."

What type of guy does Riley like? In an interview for *MTV's Buzz Worthy*, Riley said she likes nerds. More specifically, she likes guys who wear braces. "It drives me nuts," she said.

Where does Riley find her inspiration? "God is my greatest inspiration in life. And my family inspires and encourages me always. I'm really blessed."

JENNA USHKOWITZ

as Tina

J Jenna Ushkowitz plays the character of Tina Cohen-Chang, the shy, stuttering, singing Asian girl with a blue streak in her hair and a touch of punk rocker in her personality. Like her character on the show, Ushkowitz was also a member of her high school Glee Club. She attended a performance arts high school. "I was the 'Type A' theater geek and class president," Ushkowitz said. "I had to do and conquer just about

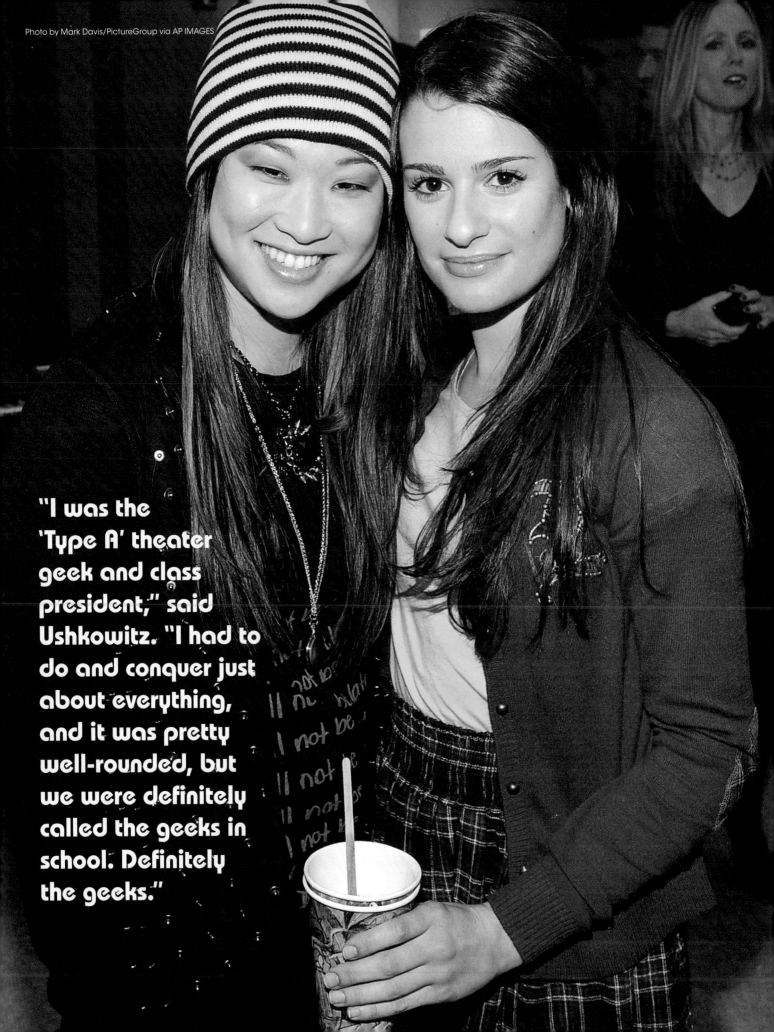

"I was the 'Type A' theater geek and class president," said Ushkowitz. "I had to do and conquer just about everything, and it was pretty well-rounded, but we were definitely called the geeks in school. Definitely the geeks."

everything, and it was pretty well-rounded, but we were definitely called the geeks in school. Definitely the geeks." Following her passion, she went on to college and minored in theatre.

Ushkowitz is an unusual name for a Korean-American actress, and that's perhaps one of the reasons her name is so recognizable. The name Ushkowitz is, in fact, Polish in origin. Young Jenna Ushkowitz was adopted from Korea when she was just three months old. Her parents quickly recognized she was an outgoing and entertaining child. They got her started in commercials and print ads at the age of three, and her interest in acting was

nurtured from a very young age.

Ushkowitz offered the following advice on pursuing your dreams, "Hard work pays off. It really does. It's very rewarding." She went on to add, "If you're happy doing what you're doing, and you work hard towards what you want, it'll pay." That certainly seems to be the case with Ushkowitz.

Prior to moving to Los Angeles to begin work on *Glee*, Ushkowitz lived in New York. *Glee* is not Ushkowitz's first foray into television acting. As a kid, she appeared on the time-honored classic children's series *Sesame Street*. With a background in theater, she also has appeared in two

Broadway shows, *The King and I* and *Spring Awakening*. She played in *Spring Awakening* alongside fellow *Glee* cast member, Lea Michele. The two have known each other since they were eight years old and have had the opportunity to work together on both Broadway and television.

Commenting on her evolving career and how she eventually landed the role of Tina, Ushkowitz told Fancast's Brian Gianelli, "I started in the *King and I*. I was on Broadway when I was nine. It kind of just kicked off from there—I went to a performing arts high school. I was a total gleek! I was in show choir, and we had acting classes during the day, dance classes during the day. But it was a Catholic school, so I did take regular classes. I went to college for it—minored in musical theater. And then I wanted to do Broadway again, so I went and did *Spring Awakening*, actually with Lea [Michele, who plays Rachel] for awhile, so that was fun. Right out of that, the casting associate out of New York for *Glee* was the casting director for *Spring Awakening*, so he saw all of us. I walked out of that audition and said, 'I didn't get that' and they called me back, and then they called me to LA and I went in for a day and I tested for the network, and Tina just kind of happened from there."

Ushkowitz was once injured

SAY ANYTHING . . .

Though quiet, shy, and sometimes stuttering on the show, Ushkowitz's character, Tina, still has some memorable lines. Here are a few of the best:

"I'm k-k-kind of nervous." (From the "Throwdown" episode.)

"I really admire you Artie. I had no idea how difficult this was." (Referring to being in a wheelchair from the "Wheels" episode.)

"All this baby drama is making my rosacea act up." (From the "Ballad" episode.)

"I can't believe we're finally breaking into the biz." (From the "Mattress" episode.)

AP Photo by Vince Bucci/PictureGroup

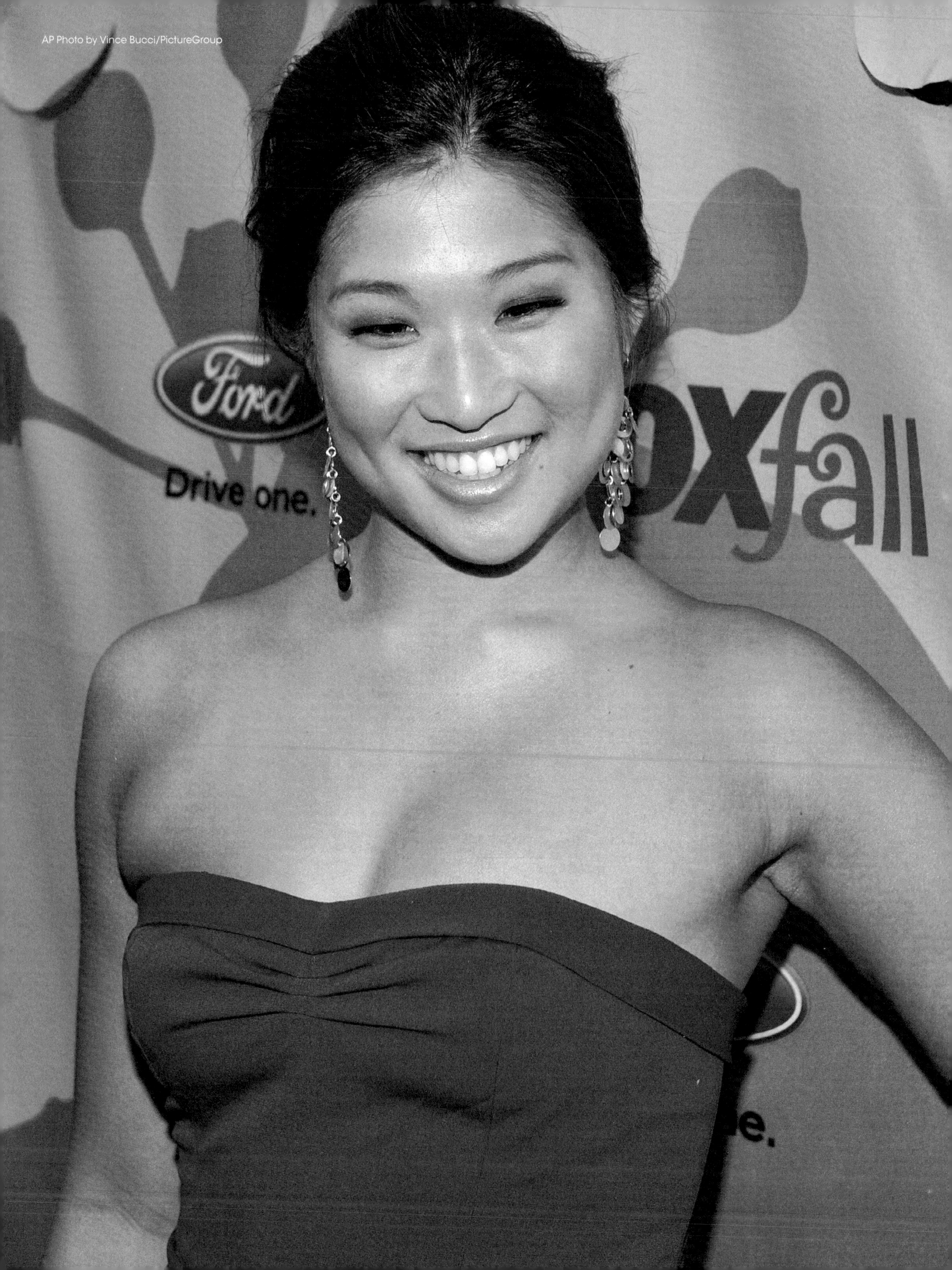

JENNA USHKOWITZ AS TINA

AP Photo T.Arroyo/JPegFoto/PictureGroup

on set when she hit her hand on a camera while filming a dance scene. "The hardest part of *Glee* in particular is that we are singing and dancing on a real stage with a camera right there in your face, following you around while you're dancing," Ushkowitz told *Seventeen* magazine. "I got whacked on my hand when I was doing 'Don't Stop Believin'.'" It was this huge bruise on the bone, it was so bad. Physically, I am afraid of the camera because we have to dodge it, and then sometimes it'll be on somebody [else] so you have to keep dancing in case they get your hand, but at the same time, you're making funny faces at the person who's on camera."

Commenting on the closeness of the *Glee* cast, Ushkowitz said, "We're best friends. We're one happy family. We have 'glee-kends,' when we bowl, we have sleepovers, and three of us actually live in the same apartment complex, so it's a little like a college dorm."

In an interview, Ushkowitz was once asked to categorize some of her castmates. She thinks that Amber Riley who plays Mercedes is the best singer, and Kevin McHale who plays Artie is the hottest. Lea Michele who plays Rachel always nails her lines, despite the fact that there are so many of them. She thinks that Cory Monteith who plays Finn is the least serious, and Chris Colfer who plays Kurt is the funniest.

Unlike the goth girl character she plays, Ushkowitz's taste in music is much more upbeat. What kind of music does Ushkowitz listen to? "Britney Spears," Ushkowitz said, "was my idol growing up. I've seen her in concert a ton of times. 'N Sync and Backstreet Boys. I was the bubblegum pop lover with the magazine cut-outs on my wall."

Ushkowitz keeps friends and fans up-to-date on Twitter. She tweets as "IJennaUsh."

What does Ushkowitz think about the success of *Glee*? "I think that it's really positive and refreshing," Ushkowitz said. "I think that it's new, and people haven't seen anything like this on TV. You have music. You have drama, a lot of love, a lot of heart, and I think that it's going to make people come back."

"The hardest part of *Glee* in particular is that we are singing and dancing on a real stage with a camera right there in your face, following you around while you're dancing."

JESSALYN GILSIG

as Terri Schuester

Jessalyn Gilsig portrays Terri Schuester, the social-climbing, pregnancy-faking, high school sweetheart wife of the Glee Club coach, Will Schuester. Gilsig, like her fellow cast member Cory Monteith, grew up in Canada. She was born in Montreal, Quebec. She received a degree in English from McGill University in Montreal, Canada, before continuing on to the prestigious American Repertory Theatre's Institute for

advanced Theatre Training at Harvard University, where she studied acting.

Gilsig starred on the television series *Boston Public* for two seasons as the straight-laced teacher Lauren Davis. She has had guest roles in several other television shows, including *To Have and To Hold, The Sentinel, The Practice, Without a Trace,* *NYPD Blue, Prison Break, Law & Order,* and *CSI: NY.* In the television series *Friday Night Lights,* she played a recurring role as Shelley Hayes.

Like her fellow cast members, Jayma Mays and Dianna Agron, Gilsig had a role in a series of episodes on the television series *Heroes.* She played Meredith Gordon, the birth mother of cheerleader Claire Bennet. Gilsig starred in ten separate episodes of *Heroes,* as a character with the special gift of pyrokinesis, the ability to start fires with just a touch of her hand and a bit of concentration.

Gilsig is no novice when it comes to playing a character that is not always nice. She also worked with *Glee* creator Ryan Murphy on his other television series, *Nip/Tuck,* in which she played the manipulative and "wildly unhinged" sex addict Gina Russo. How does Gilsig feel about playing a character who people sometimes dislike? "I'd rather play Terri than anybody else," she said. "I like the challenge, and I don't want to apologize for her. I'm learning to be at peace with it and accept that I'm not the most popular girl in the room."

In real life, Gilsig is much nicer and more down-to-earth than her high maintenance character on the show. She is happily married to a producer, and the two have a three-year-old daughter named Penelope. She said that being with her family is what makes her feel most gleeful.

Gilsig said that she was drawn to the role of Terri primarily for the opportunity to work with creator Ryan Murphy once again. "Because I had worked with him on *Nip/Tuck,*" Gilsig said. "And that was one of the best experiences as an actor

SAY ANYTHING . . .

Jessalyn Gilsig plays the character of Terri Schuester, who viewers are sometimes conflicted with, but whose lines are so memorable. Here are a few examples:

"But Will, I'm on my feet four hours a day, three times a week here."
(From the pilot episode, in reference to her part-time job.)

"Oh, it's just hamburger casserole. Look out for bones."
(From the "Acafellas" episode.)

"I don't think we've been properly introduced. I'm Terri Schuester, Will's pregnant wife."
(To Emma in the "Vitamin D" episode.)

"All the more reason you gotta do what it takes, Honey. You gotta get down in the gutter if you want to win this."
(From the "Throwdown" episode.)

"Listen you little psycho, this is Will's wife, and if I don't get enough sleep, my antidepressants won't work, and then I'll go crazy, and I'll kill you." (From the "Ballad" episode.)

"I'm taking responsibility, Will. I mean, I'm weak, and I'm selfish, and I let my anxiety rule my life, but you know I wasn't always that way. It's just that I wanted so many things that I know we're never going to have, but that was okay as long as I still had you."
(From the "Sectionals" episode.)

"I'd rather play Terri than anybody else.
I like the challenge, and I don't want to apologize for her.
I'm learning to be at peace with it and accept that I'm not

JESSALYN GILSIG AS TERRI SCHUESTER

I've ever had in my career. He really challenges you as an actor, and he really pushes you, and he really puts a lot of faith in actors to be able to—I think go further than they've ever gone before." She went on to explain in an interview for The TV Chick blog that she also welcomed the opportunity to work on a comedy, which was a nice change of pace after some of her previous television roles. "For me," Gilsig said, "the opportunity to do a comedy is something that I've been itching to do for many years now and also if I was going to do that—which is kind of a big risk for me—to be able to do that with Ryan, who I know so well, and then so much of the crew that I was familiar with

from *Nip/Tuck* was kind of a dream scenario I would say."

When asked if the massive success of *Glee* surprised her, Gilsig said, "It did and it didn't. When we were doing it, it reminded me a lot of when you're doing a play, and you think 'Something's happening here.' You could feel it, you know?"

Despite not being a member of the Glee Club, we can look forward to hearing Gilsig sing for the first time on the show. She admitted that there have been discussions about writing a song for her into an episode at some point in the future. In regards to her singing experience, Gilsig jokingly replied in an interview that her voice was so deep that she

only got to sing for male roles in high school plays.

Gilsig attended the Trafalgar School for Girls in Montreal, Canada. Commenting on how closely her own high school experiences mimicked the themes in the show, Gilsig said, "I was an art geek. I was most comfortable in art class and in theater class, so that's when I felt most like myself. And then when those classes would end, and you go back out into the hall, I was uncomfortable. I found high school kind of hard. And I knew that when I was in the arts, that was when I felt like I could be myself and I was accepted and understood and I could feel a real connection with other people. So in that way, I really relate to the show. I think it really speaks to the high school spirit. Whether or not you're in the arts or the sciences or sports or whatever it is, you hope to find that club that speaks to you."

Gilsig is not only an accomplished actress, but a painter as well. Her art work appeared in the 2003 film *The Station Agent*.

As a busy actress, Gilsig is used to juggling multiple projects. In addition to her many roles in various television shows, she was also in the miniseries *XIII* with Val Kilmer and Stephen Dorff. Gilsig has also appeared on the big screen in such movies as *The Horse Whisperer* and *The Stepfather*.

AP Photo/Jeff Christensen

LEA MICHELE

as Rachel Berry

Lea Michele portrays main character Rachel Berry, the perky, picked-on perfectionist. She is the New Directions star cast member who sings most of the female solos. With the support of her two fathers, Rachel was raised to pursue her musical performance dreams from the time she could walk and talk. She is convinced that Glee Club is one important step on her way to the top.

About her character Rachel, Michele commented, "Well, Rachel was raised by two gay men in Ohio, and I think that she grew up watching a lot of classic movies—*Funny Girl, Cabaret, West Side Story*—I definitely think that she was very much like me as a child, talking at a very young age and always putting on shows in her living room… Her fathers have taught her to be proud of who she is and comfortable in her own skin."

Show creator Ian Brennan referred to the role of Rachel as "a fantastic little fireball of a starlet who is spectacularly talented and utterly tone deaf to how she comes across to people."

In 2009, Michele appeared on the *Tyra Banks Show* and talked about how she was able to identify with her character, Rachel. "I was pretty much like Rachel Berry in high school, not so much as an outcast as she is," reported Michele, going on to talk about how she was driven in much the same way as the character she plays on *Glee*. "I knew what I wanted to be, and I knew who I was. I didn't care what other people thought, really. I knew that there was sort of a light at the end of the high school hallway, I guess, and that I wanted to perform, and that I loved to perform. And if people had a problem with that, I didn't really care."

Though Michele was singing and performing professionally from the time she was a kid, she didn't last long in her own high school choir. She managed to pursue her love for singing in other ways, such as going straight on to Broadway.

Michele had already established herself as a talented and vibrant stage actress prior to auditioning for the part of Rachel Berry. She made her Broadway debut at the age of eight-years-old in *Les Miserables*. She got the part after attending an open casting call that a friend told her about. Not only was it the first audition this young aspiring actress had ever attended, but it was the

SAY ANYTHING . . .

Lea Michele plays the intensely driven and talented Rachel Berry, whose lines on the show stand out almost as much as her spectacular singing voice. Here's a sample of some of the best Rachel quotes:

"You may think that all the boys in school would totally want to tap this, but my MySpace schedule keeps me way too busy to date." (From the pilot episode.)

"Can I use the auditorium later to practice? Our neighbors are filing a lawsuit." (From the "Showmance" episode.)

"If there's anything I've learned in my sixteen years on the stage, it's that stars are rare, and when they're found, you have to let them shine." (From "The Rhodes Not Taken" episode.)

"Let's just say, I feel sorry for my Dads because they're probably going to have to dip into my college fund to pay for intensive therapy." (From the "Throwdown" episode.)

"Maybe one of these days you'll find a way to create 'teaching moments' without ruining my life." (To Mr. Schu in the "Wheels" episode.)

"I can cry on demand. It's one of my many talents. I'm very versatile, and aside from nudity and the exploitation of animals, I'll pretty much do anything to break into the business." (From the "Mattress" episode.)

AP Photo: T.Arroyo/JPegFoto/PictureGroup

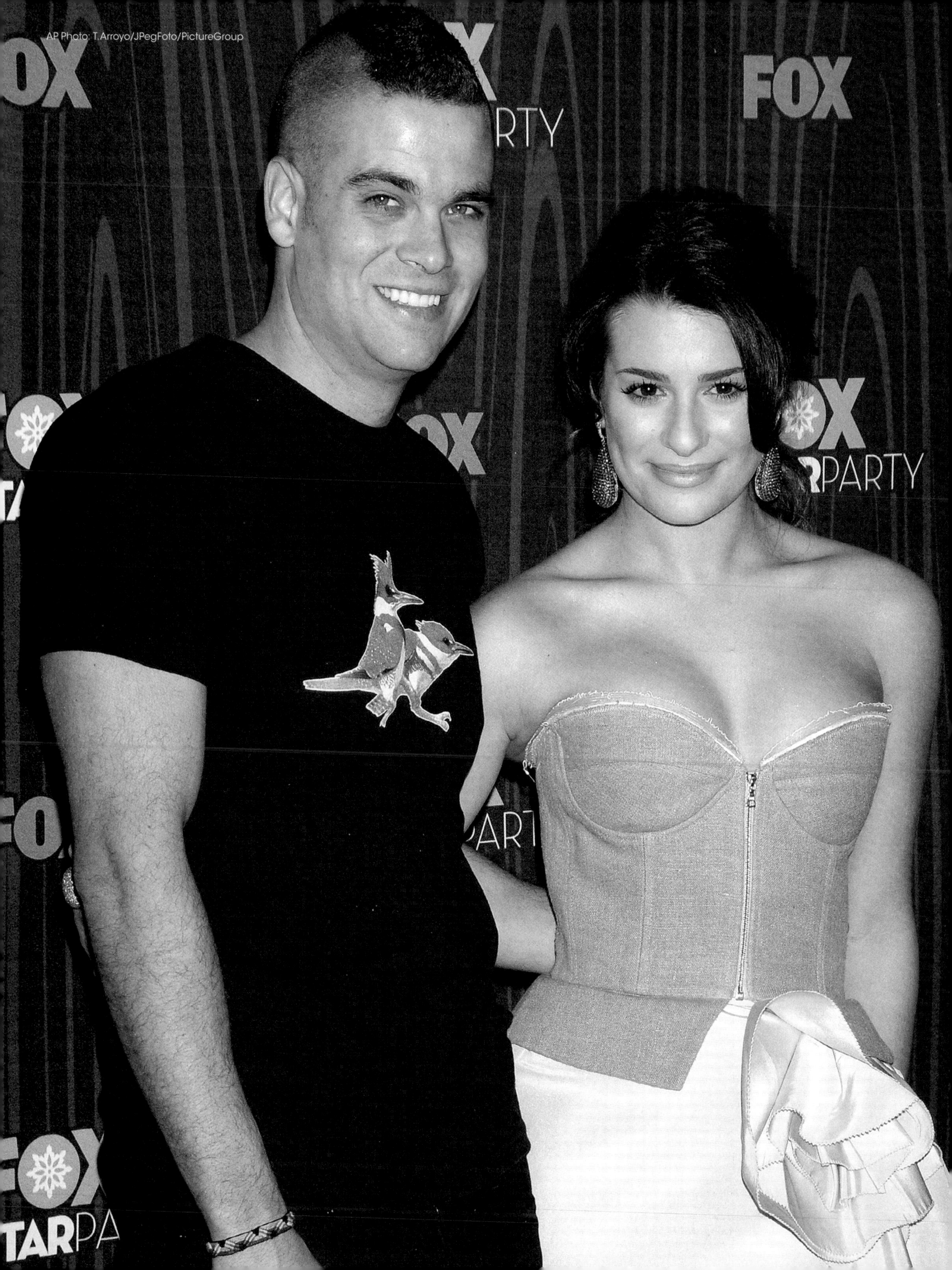

first time she had ever sung. "The first song I ever sang was in the audition of the first job that I ever got," Michele said in an interview with *The Washington Post*. "Like, literally I had never sang before, and I went on an audition for *Les Miz* on Broadway—there was an open call in my home town. And I just thought it was fun 'cause my friend was doing it, so I was like, 'Eh! I'll do it, too!' And I was a really outgoing, funny kid, so I was just like 'Yeah! What the heck?' And the only Broadway musical I'd ever seen, I'd

in eight shows per week for *Les Miserables*, while still attending elementary school.

Michele sang on Broadway again in the Tony Award–winning musical *Spring Awakening*. She played the starring role of Wendla Bergman, a teenager girl who discovers her own awakening sexuality. Michele was nominated for a Drama Desk Award in the category of Outstanding Actress in a Musical. She also appeared on Broadway in *Fiddler on the Roof* and *Ragtime*, and she appeared in one episode of

regular tweets on Twitter as "msleamichele." She posts about her time on the set and upcoming appearances.

During the round of various awards shows this season, Michele established herself on the red carpet as a sophisticated fashionista whose designer gowns were not only elegant and flattering, but also reflected her personality. She commented in an interview with E! that she was with her mother and her *Spring Awakening* co-star, Jonathan Groff, when she found out that she had been nominated for a Golden Globe Award, which made it extra special because she and her mother used to dress up each year just to watch the awards shows together at home. She brought her mother as her date to the Golden Globes ceremony.

In January 2010, Michele presented the award for Best Female Pop Vocalist at the 52nd Annual Grammy Awards to Beyoncé for her song "Halo." Coincidentally, prior to the Grammy Awards show, Michele along with the other female members of the *Glee* cast performed a cover of Beyoncé's song "Halo" on the "Vitamin D" episode of *Glee*.

In an interview for Australian TV, Michele spoke about her long days on the set and her love for what she does. "If it wasn't so fun, we would have been so burnt out, and

> **"I think as actors, I think I speak for everyone when I say that we feel really lucky to be a part of such a well written show that has such incredible characters. For actors, it's like, it's a dream to be working, but also to be working on something this good."**

gone to a week earlier—it was *Phantom of the Opera*. And I was mesmerized—I remember sitting on the edge of my seat, loving it. And I listened to the CD at home, and I was able to pick up the sounds and learn the song, and I was in the audition room and the first song I ever sang was "Angel of Music," and I haven't stopped singing since." She performed

the television series *Third Watch* prior to making the full time transition from Broadway to television.

Michele told David Letterman on *The Late Show*, "You know, I decided at a really young age that this is what I wanted to do and it's what I loved, and so I've been kind of doing it ever since." Michele keeps fans up to date with

it would have been really hard," Michele said. She went on to add, "It's the days that are the hardest, but I feel the most energized afterwards because they literally fill me up. They make me so happy." In the interview, Michele's facial expressions and hand gestures were very animated, conveying such enthusiasm in reaction to this particular topic, that it was clear that she was genuinely excited about all her hard work on the show.

In fact, Michele loves what she does so much that she manages to grin and bear it when it comes to physical pain, all in the name of professional dedication. The young actress suffered a back injury while filming that was significant enough to result in recur-

BABY YOU CAN DRIVE MY CAR

On her way to her second audition, Michele got into a major car accident. Determined to play the role of Rachel, she was not about to let that stop her from auditioning. Though she was "literally still pulling pieces of glass" from her hair when she arrived at her audition, she still managed to "wow" the casting directors. She sang "On My Own" from *Les Misera-bles*, which was written into the pilot show for her to sing. She pulled several very "Rachel" maneuvers during her audition, such as asking the pianist to start over from the beginning because he skipped the second verse of her song and repri-manding the casting directors for laughing during her serious moment.

ring painful muscle spasms. "We all did this one dance number a couple of weeks ago that was extremely grueling," Michele said. "Now I have back spasms every so often. I'll be talking and be like, 'Excuse

me a minute,' and my back will just spaz out. And then I'll be fine. But we ignore it because we're all just happy doing what we do. We don't pay attention to our injuries." It's clear that Michele is one tough cookie,

LEA MICHELE AS RACHEL BERRY

willing to sacrifice for her art.

Commenting on how much fun it is to work on *Glee*, Michele told talk show host Bonnie Hunt, "We're having a blast. I mean, not only are we having so much fun together, we're just really really proud to be a part of a show that we all believe in so much."

The cast members of *Glee* are all friends and spend a lot of their free time hanging out together. Michele and fellow *Glee* cast member, Dianna Agron who plays Quinn Fabray, are roommates in Los Angeles. They are both vegetarians and enjoy cooking

at home to unwind. While the *Glee* cast was in Chicago, Michele tried to talk her fellow cast members into getting matching tattoos together. The only two who agreed were Kevin McHale who plays Artie and Jenna Ushkowitz who plays Tina. The three friends got "Imagine" tattooed in different places. Michele's is on her foot. McHale's is on his leg, and Ushkowitz had hers done on her arm. Colfer who plays Kurt came along for the ride and supported his cast mates while they got their tattoos, but said that he was too afraid of all those needles to get one of

his own.

Michele offered the following advice to high school students: "It doesn't matter, like, where you are or what clique you're in, who your friends are. Really, what matters the most is that you're doing what you love to do and that you do well in school. I know that sounds really cheesy, but it's just like nothing else matters. Doing the things that you love to do, whether it's playing sports or being in drama or whatever, and to do well because that's really important."

Ever wonder what the talented soloist of *Glee* prefers for music? In addition to the many show tunes and ballads she performs on the show, she claims to "really love classic rock." When asked what was on her iPod, her response was "Queen, The Who, Journey, all of that. Then the next track will come on, and it will be 'Don't Rain on My Parade.'" She said that Celine Dion, Barbara Streisand, and Alanis Morrisette are her "idols."

When asked whether or not she ever thought there would be a television show that would allow her to sing and act in the way that she does on *Glee*, Michele responded, "No, honestly, I never ever thought that there would be a television show that I felt sort of catered to what I feel I do well and a character that's as fun as her."

AP Photo: S.Bergman/JPegFoto/PictureGroup

In its first season, *Glee* produced two gold soundtracks and four million iTunes downloads.

Sing, Sing a Song

Glee Success Fueling The Musical Dreams Of The Show's Fans

The phenomenal success of the *Glee* hit factory and its interpretation of covers is dominating the Billboard charts, iTunes, and YouTube. With more than four million iTunes downloads of *Glee* song selections and two volumes of soundtrack CDs that have both hit gold status selling more than 500,000 copies each, the unique interpretations of familiar songs are certainly in demand. *Glee* helped Journey's "Don't Stop Believin'" hit No. 1 on iTunes downloads shortly after the pilot episode aired, making it the only song on the iTunes Top 25 most downloaded songs list that had not been released in the past five years. As of February 2010, three of the top 25 most downloaded songs on iTunes ("I Kissed a Girl" by Katy Perry, "Single Ladies" by Beyoncé, and "Don't Stop Believin'" by Journey) were songs that had been covered on *Glee*. The music of *Glee* has become a phenomenon in and of itself, and *Glee* songs are topping the charts across both the U.S. and the U.K.

In the "Sectionals" episode of *Glee*, there was a tongue-in-cheek line about "Don't Stop Believin'" being "the most downloaded song in the history of iTunes." The fact that *Glee* helped solidify that fact after the number was performed in the pilot

The Sound of Music is one of many American musicals that are successful both on stage and film.

episode, makes the line a bit of a tip-of-the-hat to its own accomplishment.

The success of *Glee* has served as inspiration for some schools to start Glee Clubs of their own. The music is even inspiring dance club parties, such as the "OMGlee" event at the Vlada club in New York City, hosted by Cheer New York, which featured DJ Raymond spinning *Glee*'s soundtrack hits, performances by Cheer New York cheerleaders, a *Glee* trivia contest, and fans taking their turn in the spotlight singing karaoke of their favorite *Glee* tunes.

When the cast of *Glee* appeared in New York City to sign copies of the newly released *Glee* soundtrack CD, hundreds of fans showed up screaming their enthusiasm. The music of *Glee* has made almost as big a splash as the television show itself.

Why is everyone so fascinated with *Glee*? Perhaps one reason is the appeal of the musical in general. America's fascination with recent hit musical entertainment productions like *High School Musical, American Idol*, and *America's Got Talent* have helped to cement musical entertainment into the hearts

of today's generation of viewers, though the roots of the American musical can be traced back to stage and the silver screen.

Stage musicals, such as the famous Broadway productions, have drawn audiences from around the globe for years. Early stage performances began in vaudeville, which allowed separate acts of entertainment to be performed under one roof. An evening of vaudeville might have included a series of singing and dancing, juggling, magic, and comedy acts. People have always looked

Katy Perry

Taylor Swift

SING, SING A SONG

to musical performances as a means of escape and entertainment.

Full length stage plays and movies that tell a story through a series of related songs are considered musicals. Musical theater has been around for decades, but it's height of success began in the 1940s, and new productions continue to be presented today. Though this genre has spanned more than a century and is widely varied, a small sample of some of the famous stage musicals would include *West Side Story*, *A Chorus Line*, *Cabaret*, *My Fair Lady*, *Evita*, *Sweeney Todd*, *Hair*, *Jesus Christ Superstar*, *Cats*, *The Phantom of the Opera*, *Les Miserables*, and *Rent*.

In addition to pop hits, *Glee* features a wide sampling of songs from famous musicals. Examples include "Sit Down You're Rocking the Boat" from *Guys and*

The cast of *Cats*.

Dolls, "Tonight" from *West Side Story*, "Maybe This Time" from *Cabaret*, "Hair" from *Hair*, "Defying Gravity" from *Wicked*, "And I Am Telling You" from *Dreamgirls*, and "Don't Rain on My Parade"

from *Funny Girl*.

To feed the interest of fans, many Broadway musicals have been adapted as movies, and original musical films have also been produced. Early musical films that captured the hearts of audiences include *Singin' in the Rain* starring Gene Kelly, Donald O'Connor, and Debbie Reynolds, *Easter Parade* starring Fred Astaire and Judy Garland, *The Wizard of Oz* starring Judy Garland, *The King and I* starring Deborah Kerr and Yul Brynner, and *The Sound of Music* starring Julie Andrews.

There have also been movie musicals that have

FAMOUS GLEEKS

Famous music icons from Madonna to Taylor Swift have declared themselves gleeks. Madonna released the rights for her entire music library to the television show, allowing the creators of *Glee* to choose any songs they'd like from her almost twenty-five year run as one of the most successful singers in history. "The Power of Madonna" episode is slated for the latter half of Season One. After covering the Amy Winehouse song "Rehab," the singer gave a shout-out Twitter tweet that began with "How cool is *Glee*?"

Wicked, a recent popular musical with gleeks, continues to generate huge audiences and sold-out performances.

SING, SING A SONG

later been produced as stage performances. Several Disney animated films that featured musical numbers, such as *Beauty and the Beast* and *The Lion King*, transitioned well from film to stage.

Many of the soundtracks from Disney films sold well, and some of the CD soundtracks included additional songs by pop music stars such as Elton John, Vanessa Williams, and Jon Secada.

West Side Story has been produced as both a stage musical and a musical film. It features teens from opposite sides of the tracks who fall in love despite their cultural differences and the pressure from family and friends to keep them apart. It was a modern musical interpretation that was adapted from Shakespeare's play *Romeo and Juliet*. Like *Romeo and Juliet*, the story and the star-crossed lovers end in tragedy, showing that not all musicals end with "happily ever after."

Many of the *Glee* cast members began pursuing their dreams of performing early on in life. Matthew Morrison, who plays Will Schuester, attended a theater camp as a kid and performed in musical theater throughout high school. Jayma Mays, who plays Emma, sang in her church choir. Jenna Ushkowitz, who plays Tina, was involved in musical theater through her school. Mark Salling, who plays Puck, performed in a rock band, and Kevin McHale, who plays Artie, performed in a boy band. Chris Colfer, who plays Kurt, was involved in community theater and school plays. Amber Riley, who plays Mercedes, took singing lessons while growing up, and Lea Michele, who plays Rachel, went straight to Broadway while she was still a child.

AP Photo/Dima Gavrysh

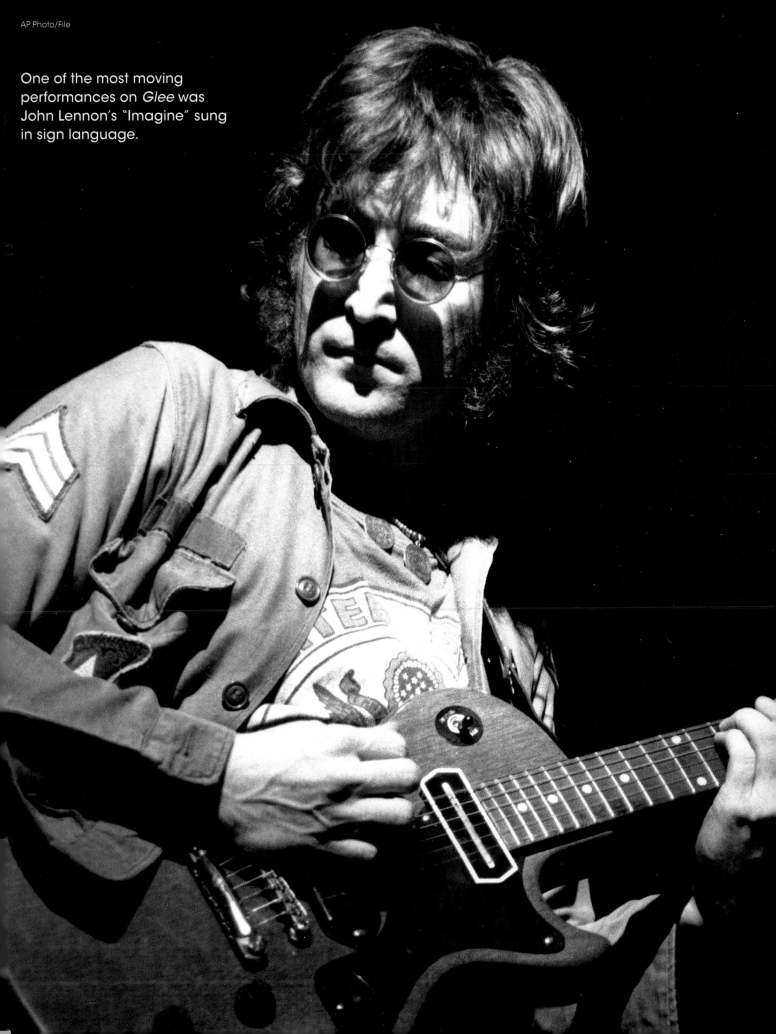

One of the most moving performances on *Glee* was John Lennon's "Imagine" sung in sign language.

SING, SING A SONG

What are some of the best ways to get started in singing or acting? There are many avenues towards exploring your talent. If you are still a student, getting started in your school's music program is one great way to develop your talent while learning to perform in front of audiences. Many park districts offer theater classes beginning as early as age three. Local communities in big cities as well as in small rural settings

Be willing to take risks and put yourself out there. Go on casting calls and auditions, whether it's for a school play or for Broadway.

often offer community theater programs, as well. Most churches offer music programs for children and adults with opportunities to participate in choirs. There are also camp programs specifically designed for

musical performance, and countless colleges and universities across the country offer drama, music, and theater departments.

Emmy award–winning actress, comedienne, talk show host, author, and producer Rosie O'Donnell has founded the nonprofit organization Rosie's Broadway Kids that helps provide underprivileged youth with opportunities to learn about and participate in musical theater. Over 80 percent of the children in her program come from families living below the poverty line, and many of them attend schools that offer no arts programs. With Tony Award–winners volunteering their time towards the program, Rosie's Broadway Kids offers once-in-a-lifetime opportunities to grow and develop an appreciation for musical theater. The main goal of Rosie's Broadway Kids is to instill a sense of hope and confidence in children that theater performance and the arts can help to impart. O'Donnell claims, "It's the thing I think I'm most proud of in my career. Honestly."

Pursuing your dream and

AP Photo/ Jan Bauer

Beauty and the Beast on Broadway.

SING, SING A SONG

Photo courtesy of Theatre On The Hill

If you are still a student, getting started in your school's music program or community theater is one great way to develop your talent while learning to perform in front of audiences. Local communities in big cities as well as in small rural settings often offer community theater programs.

performing doesn't necessarily require an ear for music. Perhaps one of the most touching *Glee* songs was a performance where the number began in sign language rather than harmonized vocals. In the "Hairography" episode, a school for the deaf performed "Imagine" by John Lennon. The McKinley High New Directions choir joined their competition in song, adding their own vocals to the sign language for a combined effect that made quite an emotional impact.

Taking classes is another

good way to get your feet wet and learn a new skill. Whether it's through a school drama department, a local park district, or a community program, taking music lessons, acting classes, or vocal lessons can help to develop your talent. Learning to play an instrument and forming a band is another good way to get involved in performance. Most communities offer Battle of the Bands contests for amateur teen groups.

Be willing to take risks and put yourself out there. Go on casting calls and auditions, whether it's for a school play

or for Broadway. Seek agent representation, which can help get your foot in the door for television and film auditions. Be willing to practice and work hard to get better. Sing out loud and read script lines with a partner. Surround yourself with people who share similar interests and support your dreams. Find a mentor, someone who has some knowledge about your area of interest, whether it's a teacher or a peer who has simply been performing longer. Most of all, believe in yourself, pursue your dreams, and do what you love.

First lady Michelle Obama, top, poses for a group photo after a special preview for local Glee Club students from Myrtilla Miner Elementary School in Washington of the talent performing at the White House.

AP Photo/Peter Kramer

Into the Future

Idina Menzel

Take a Sneak Peek at Some of the Possible *Glee* Guest Stars

This chapter contains spoilers. If you don't want to be spoiled rotten, then feel free to skip this chapter. However, if you're a gleek who can't wait to catch a glimpse of some of the juicy things *Glee* has in store, then this is the chapter for you.

Glee has already featured some amazing guest stars in its first season, and there are many more still to come. Victor Garber and Josh Groban

were the first big guest stars to make appearances on *Glee*. They were both in the "Acafellas" episode, in which Garber played the role of Will Schuester's father. Groban didn't sing, perform, or have a fictional role written into the storyline. Instead, he made a brief cameo appearance as himself at the end of the show.

Kristin Chenoweth won a Satellite Special Achievement Award as an Outstanding Guest Star for her work on *Glee*.

She played April Rhodes, the saucy character who returned to high school under the guise of completing her degree yet with the primary intention of shining in the spotlight as the female soloist for the New Directions Glee Club. Actor Mark Salling, who plays Puck, called Chenoweth "a doll—literally and figuratively," and said that he kept messing up the scene in "The Rhodes Not Taken" episode where Chenoweth kisses him, implying that he was enjoying the retakes quite a bit. She is scheduled to reappear in her continuing guest role of April Rhodes. Chenoweth's list of acting credits are nearly

Kristin Chenoweth

endless, but she is perhaps best known for her television roles of Olive Snook in *Pushing Daisies* and Annabeth Schott in *The West Wing,* and for her Broadway role as Glinda in *Wicked.*

Actress and comedienne Molly Shannon is expected to appear on *Glee.* The former *Saturday Night Live* "superstar" cast member will play a character named Brenda Castle, a McKinley High astronomy teacher and badminton coach who is rarely seen sober. She will be one more in the growing list of Coach Sue's enemies and adversaries. In addition to playing roles in movies such as *Never Been Kissed, Superstar, Shallow Hal,* and *Serendipity,* Shannon recently starred in the comedy television series *Kath and Kim.*

Wicked Broadway star Idina Menzel is slated to guest star in a recurring role on multiple episodes. During the second portion of Season One, she will play Will Schuester's rival, as the coach of the "Vocal Adrenaline" show choir. Much to the disappointment of "Wemma" fans, there have been hints of a potential romantic entanglement between the two Glee Club coaches.

Another Broadway star, Jonathan Groff, will appear in the latter portion of Season One. He will be playing the male lead vocalist for the rival "Vocal Adrenaline" Glee Club,

Beyoncé

WHO WOULD WE LIKE TO SEE ON *GLEE?*

There are so few triple threats who can sing, dance, and act, but here's a list of a few that would be spectacular as dream guest stars on the show:

CHER

Like Madonna, this one-name wonder is a music icon who would make for a very memorable episode. Perhaps they could incorporate a few of her original songs into the show and have her appear in a cameo spot as herself.

HUGH JACKMAN

He can sing and dance. He's starred on Broadway, hosted the Academy Awards, and played *X-Men*'s Wolverine. He's got it all and would make a great Glee Club choreographer. Maybe he'd give Mr. Schu a little run for his money?

WILL SMITH

He's made a career as both an actor and a rapper. He'd be great in a guest cameo as a geek chic McKinley High substitute teacher.

ALICIA KEYS

In the movie *The Secret Life of Bees*, Keyes showed audiences that she was an actress as well as the keeper of a sultry soulful voice. Perhaps she could make an appearance as a pianist hired to help the "New Directions" prepare for a big competition.

EWAN MCGREGOR

Since starring in the movie *Moulin Rouge*, McGregor established himself as a true triple threat. He'd make a great love interest, competing with Will for Emma's affections.

QUEEN LATIFAH

She can sing and act like nobody's business. Can't you just picture her playing the role of Mercedes' Mom?

HILARY DUFF

The actress and pop star Hilary Duff would make a great soloist in a rival Glee Club or maybe even a Cheerios cheerleader.

BEYONCÉ KNOWLES

Perhaps she could do a rendition duet with Kurt singing "Single Ladies."

INTO THE FUTURE

and he'll be auditioning for the role of Rachel Berry's boyfriend. Groff and Lea Michele, who plays Rachel, are very close and spend much of their time together. The two also co-starred together on Broadway in *Spring Awakening*.

Singer and actress Olivia Newton-John will be guest starring on an episode of *Glee*. She'll sing a duet with Jane Lynch in her role as Cheerios Coach Sue Sylvester. They'll be singing Olivia Newton-John's song "Physical." As the star of the movie *Grease*, Newton-John has quite a bit of experience singing in a musical that is set in a high school. "I'm so excited I can't see straight!" Lynch told E!, adding that Newton-John "provided the soundtrack for my tortured adolescence. Her charitable work and commitment to making others' lives and the life of the planet better is so inspiring."

In the latter half of Season One, there will be an episode entirely dedicated to the music of Madonna. The episode will feature approximately ten Madonna songs and is aptly titled "The Power of Madonna." *Glee* creator Ryan Murphy was vague about whether or not Madonna would make a cameo appearance in the episode, but the singer and songwriter generously opened up the rights to her entire collection of music for use by *Glee*.

It seems likely that pop singer and actress Jennifer Lopez may also make a guest star appearance on *Glee*, possibly wearing a very uncharacteristic hair net and serving up cafeteria food. "I have a meeting with Jennifer Lopez in a couple weeks," Ryan Murphy told reporters at the Golden Globes award ceremony. "She wants to come on. We want her to be a cafeteria lady."

Neil Patrick Harris, who plays Barney Stinson on *How I Met Your Mother*, will be guest starring in episode 19 of Season One. Harris is well known for his singing talent. Some of his musical credits include the internet miniseries *Dr. Horrible's Sing-Along Blog*, the stage musical *Sweeney Todd*, and Broadway productions of *Assassins*, *Proof*, and *Cabaret*. He hosted the 2009 Tony Awards. Like many of the *Glee* cast, Harris began singing and acting early on in life. He sang and performed in high school musicals at La Cueva High School in Albuquerque, NM, and he starred in the television series *Doogie Howser, M.D.* while he was still a teen.

Joss Whedon, the creator of the popular television series *Buffy the Vampire Slayer*, *Angel*, *Firefly*, and *Dollhouse*, will be a guest director on *Glee*. He will be directing the episode in which Neil Patrick Harris will guest star. Whedon also directed Harris in the online

Neil Patrick Harris

AP Photo/Mark J. Terrill

miniseries, *Dr. Horrible's Sing-Along Blog*.

Who would the cast of *Glee* like to see as guest stars on the show? Lea Michele, who plays Rachel, said that she would like to see Justin Timberlake as a guest star. "Aside from being an incredible singer and dancer, he's also a fantastic comedic actor, and that is a great

cocktail for being on *Glee*," she told E! "And I think he and Matt [Morrison] (who plays Glee Club director, Will Schuester, would have a fantastic dance-off."

When asked who her dream guest star would be, actress Dianna Agron, who plays Quinn Fabray, replied, "It might never happen, but I'm just gonna

INTO THE FUTURE

Madonna and Justin Timberlake

AP Photo/Mark J. Terrill

keep saying this: Christopher Walken. I think he would be amazing. He's so funny and I'm sure he can sing as well as he can dance." Amber Riley, who plays Mercedes, said, "I would love if Patti LaBelle came on the show. She's one of my favorite artists of all time."

With numerous awards already under its belt, combined with its fanatically gleeky following, it's no surprise that *Glee* received an early renewal notice for a second season. What can we expect to see in Season Two? Along with inspired new renditions of popular hits and show tunes, three new characters are on the way!

Did you think it was possible to steal the spotlight away

from Rachel Berry? One of the three new characters is going to give it her best shot. Murphy described her as "sort of an Eve Harrington" from the 1950 Bette Davis movie *All About Eve*, which depicts a young and deviously ambitious actress who positions herself into the life of a Broadway star in order to shove the reigning diva aside in her own pursuit of stardom. This classic set-up of overconfident star and scheming understudy shall provide an engaging storyline for the new season ahead.

The second new role to debut in Season Two will be a boyfriend for character Kurt Hummel. They're looking to cast someone athletic and good looking. Murphy reported that

they're going to be "a power couple. We're not going to do the whole 'hiding in the shadows' thing. We're going to make them popular and out and proud and glamorous. Like prom king and king. We're doing the *opposite* of what's been done." This move should both entertain fans and give critics more fodder with the addition of a gay teenage pairing. Watch out McKinley High—sounds like Kurt and his new BF are about to make a splash as the school's new "It" couple.

Finally, the third new role for Season Two will be what Murphy referred to as "a male Mercedes." He'll sing R&B hits and will give gleeks more of the attitude and charm admired so much in Mercedes. Will this new chemistry prove combustible or will there be love in store for Mercedes and this new Season Two character? With a sly smile, Murphy said, "Perhaps." Guess we'll just have to watch and see!

These new characters will serve as a big break for three unknown actors. Despite portraying high school students, aspiring actors and singing hopefuls between the ages of 16 and 26 have been invited to audition for the roles by submitting audition videos. *Glee* creator Ryan Murphy said, "*Glee* has always been about finding new fresh exciting voices."

Fan The Flames

An Insider's Guide to Gleek Gossip

Where are the best places to go for all the gleeky gossip, show trivia, episode reviews, facts about the *Glee* cast, and spoilers about what's to come? (Well, besides this book, of course...) Here's a list of a few great resources.

"The Ausiello Files" section of *Entertainment Weekly*, which can be found at ausiellofiles. ew.com, is a great source for all the latest television scoops. Michael Ausiello recently reported that the *Glee* cast have been invited to perform at the White House for the annual Easter Egg roll, which will be held on April 5, 2010.

BlogCritics Magazine, which can be found at blogcritics. org, is a great place to go for episode reviews and show commentary. You can also find reviews of the *Glee* music releases and news articles related to the show at this informative site.

E! is a hot source for the latest happenings on the *Glee* set. Kristin Dos Santos of E!'s "Watch with Kristin" has hosted several exclusive interviews with the cast members of *Glee*. Articles and videos can be accessed online at eonline. com.

The *Glee* website hosted by FOX, which can be found at fox.com/glee, is a great place to go to see photos of the *Glee* cast and video extras, such as audition videos and full episodes that have recently been aired. You can also find the music listed by episode and community discussion forums. It's the place to go for

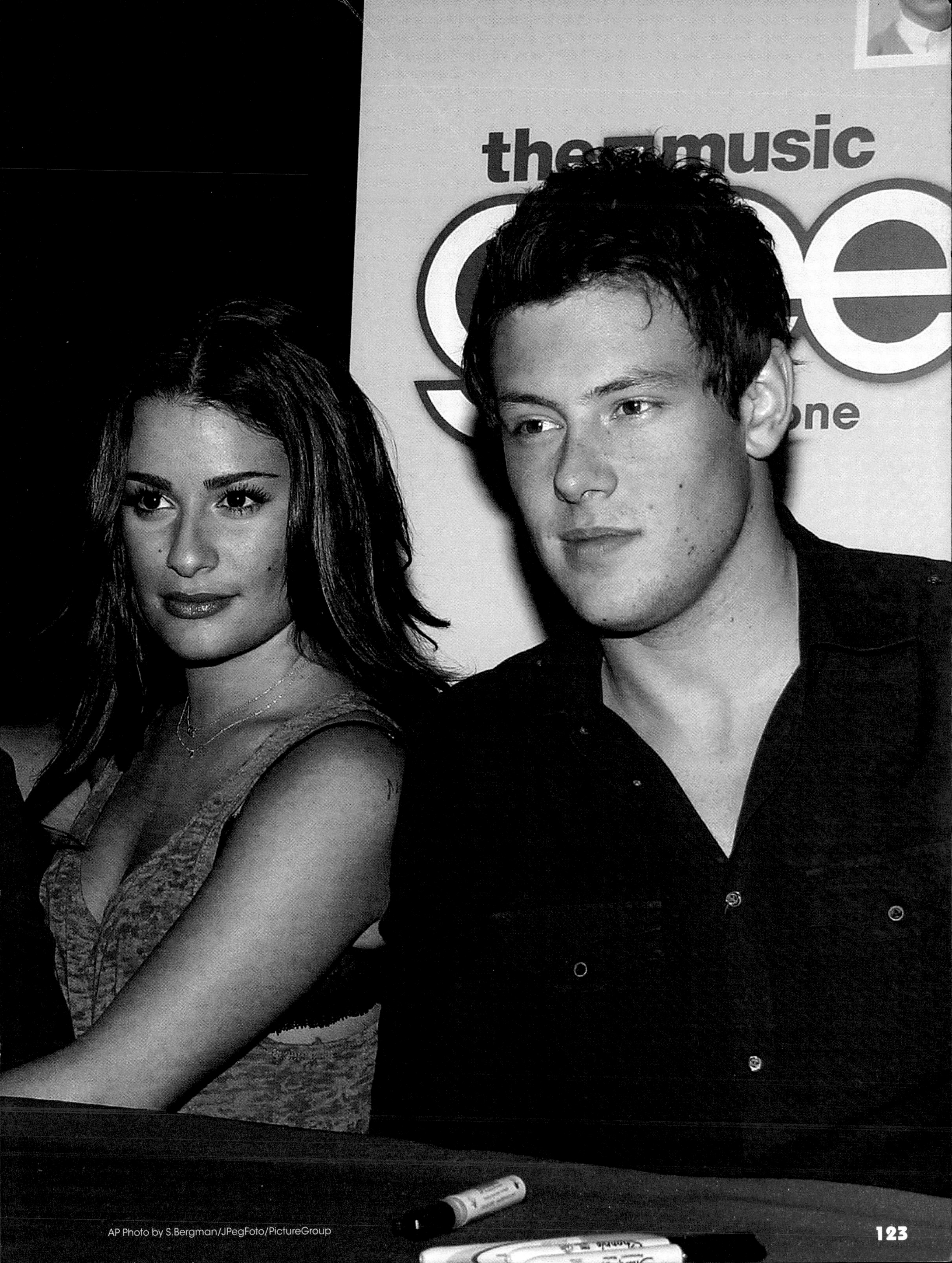

AP Photo by S.Bergman/JPegFoto/PictureGroup

information about the upcoming video audition casting call to fill the slots for the three new characters who will join the show in Season Two. The FOX *Glee* Wiki site, which can be found at gleewiki.fox.com, is a source for fans featuring the Glee Club blog and show trivia.

GleeFan.com is a great *Glee* fan site and blog that posts news about the show and the actors who play our favorite "New Directions" show choir.

Perez Hilton is the true "gossip girl" of Hollywood. His web site, perezhilton.com, boasts "celebrity juice, not from concentrate" and has information on all the hottest Hollywood celebs, including, of course, the cast of *Glee*.

The TV Chick blog, which can be found at thetvchick. com, features news and reviews on all things television-related. There are several exclusive interviews with cast members from *Glee*. The tag line for this blog is "TV from the inside out."

Young Hollywood has aired several interviews with *Glee* cast members, along with other news stories, which can all be accessed at younghollywood.com.

Glee can also be found on Facebook at facebook. com/glee and on MySpace at myspace.com/gleeonfox.

Photo by Jordan Strauss/Getty Images

BIBLIOGRAPHY

Articles, Interviews, and DVDs:

Anderson, Eric. "'Glee' Star Matthew Morrison Reveals Plans for Solo Album." *Access Hollywood.* 27 Oct 2009.

Associated Press. "'Glee' episode irks advocates for disabled." *The Hollywood Reporter.* 10 Nov 2009.

Associated Press. "*Glee*'s Jenna Ushkowitz Dishes on the Show and her Fellow Gleeks!" *Seventeen.* 6 Nov 2009.

Ausiello, Michael. "Exclusive: 'Glee' boss on Rachel/Puck, Kurt's new BF, and Madonna!" *Entertainment Weekly.* 18 Jan 2010.

Ausiello, Michael. "Exclusive: President Obama orders a command performance by the 'Glee' kids." *Entertainment Weekly.* 22 Feb 2010.

Ausiello, Michael. "'Glee' exclusive: Molly Shannon declares war on Sue Sylvestor." *Entertainment Weekly.* 10 Feb 2010.

Ausiello, Michael. "'Glee' Exclusive: Third Mystery Role Revealed." *Entertainment Weekly.* 28 Jan 2010.

Boursaw, Jane. "Jimmy Fallon Gets a 'Glee'-Inspired Idea." *AOL Television.* 2 Feb 2010.

Cohen, Corine. "An Interview with Matthew Morrison." *Corine's Corner.* Date unknown.

Daw, Robbie. "How Many of iTunes' 25 Most-Downloaded Songs Do You Own?" *Idolator.* 12 Feb 2010.

DiNunno, Gina. "*Glee*'s Matthew Morrison to 'Bust a Move.'" *TVGuide.com.* 8 Sep 2009.

Dos Santos, Kristin. "*Glee* Boss Gets on Board with Puck and Rachel!" *E! Online.* 10 Nov 2009.

Dos Santos, Krisitin. "*Glee*'s Jane Lynch on Guest Star Olivia Newton-John: 'I'm So Excited I Can't See Straight!'" 11 Jan 2010.

Duran, Rick. "Role Models – Jane Lynch Interview." *The Frat Pack Tribute.* 2008.

Eastman, Marc. "Glee's Jane Lynch Interview." *TV.com.* 11 Jan 2010.

Fernandez, Maria Elena. "Chris Colfer's journey from small town to 'Glee.'" *Los Angeles Times.* 8 Sep 2009.

Freydkin, Donna. "Baby-faced Chris Colfer leaps into 'Glee,' his acting target." *USA Today.* 13 Nov 2009.

Gianelli, Brian. "5 Questions with 'Glee's' Jenna Ushkowitz." *Fancast Tuned In.* 8 Sep 2009.

Glee: Season 1, Vol. 1, Road to Sectionals. 20th Century Fox. 2009.

Goldman, Andrew. "Matthew Morrison: The music man has moves to make Timberlake blush." *Elle.* 18 Dec 2009.

Hater, Hilton. "Taylor Swift and Cory Monteith: New Couple Alert?" *The Hollywood Gossip.* 1 Feb 2010.

Holbrook, Damian. "Exclusive: Lea Michele Shares Her *Glee*." *TV Guide Magazine.* 27 Oct 2009.

House, M.L. "Glee Casting for Trio of New Roles." *TV Fanatic.* 12 Jan 2010.

Kaplan, Ben. "Cory Monteith from Glee eschews those nasty rumours about his on-screen co-star Lea Michele." *National Post.* 17 Nov 2009.

Keck, William. "*Glee* is Moving to *Cleveland*." *TV Guide Magazine.* 7 Jan 2010.

Leal, Fermin. "School boasts grads from 'Glee' to Broadway." *The Orange County Register.* 4 Nov 2009.

Masello, Robert. "The star of the hit TV show Glee Matthew Morrison has big dreams: 'I Want To Do It All.'" *Parade.* 29 Nov 2009.

McCann, Ruth. "An Interview With Lea Michele, One of the Leads in Fox's 'Glee'." *The Washington Post.* 6 Sep 2009.

McNamara, Mary. "'Glee' on Fox." *Los Angeles Times.* 19 May 2009.

O'Connor, Mickey. "Ryan Murphy on *Glee*." *TV Guide.* 19 May 2009.

Portantiere, Michale. "*Naked* Boy, Not Singing." *Theater Mania.* 14 Sep 2005.

Reiher, Andrea. "'Glee:' Lea Michele greets and tweets Idina Menzel." *Zap 2 News & Buzz from Inside the Box.* 21 Jan 2010.

Salamone, Gina. "Jennifer Lopez may join Madonna as 'Glee' guest star – as a cafeteria lady." *New York Daily News.* 19 Jan 2010.

Tennis, Joe. "Living a Hollywood Dream." *Bristol Herald Courier.* 15 Feb 2009.

Tom & Lorenzo. "Gleeful Woman." *Metro Source.* Jan 2010.

Warn, Sarah. "Interview with Jane Lynch." *After Ellen.* 15 Nov 2004.

BIBLIOGRAPHY

Waterman, Lauren. "Dianna Agron." *Interview.* Jan 2010.

Zinn, Esther. "Wedding Bells in May for Jane Lynch and Lara Embry." *Go Magazine.* 27 Jan 2010.

Zuckerman, Suzanne. "Dreaming Big: Dianna Agron of Glee." *Women's Health.* 28 Jan 2010.

Web Site Data & Video Clips

http://www.buddytv.com/articles/cory-monteith/exclusive-video-interview-chri-31550.aspx

http://www.dipity.com/timeline/glee

http://www.fanpop.com/spots/glee/videos/6426365/title/glee-kevin-mchale-arty-chris-colfer-kurt

http://www.fanpop.com/spots/glee/videos/6426216/title/glee-mark-salling-puck

http://www.gleefan.com/gleefan-exclusive-amber-riley-qa/

http://www.hulu.com

http://iamkoream.com/jenna-ushkowitz/

http://www.ibdb.com

http://www.imdb.com

http://www.jsyk.com/2009/12/02/exclusive-interview-slushies-and-tweets-with-the-glee-cast/

http://justjared.buzznet.com/2009/11/04/mark-salling-interview/

http://marksallingmusic.com

http://www.nextmagazine.com/events/omglee

http://www.people.com/people/videos/0,,20302701,00.html

http://perezhilton.com/2010-02-18-glee-injury

http://www.popeater.com/2009/11/09/kevin-mchale-glee-wheelchair/

http://www.popeater.com/2009/11/10/glee-cast-dish-on-musical-influences-satans-gift-to-earth/

http://www.radaronline.com/exclusives/2009/10/exclusive-video-interview-glees-mark-salling-talks-music-mohawks-kissing-kristin

http://www.radaronline.com/exclusives/2009/10/video-glees-matthew-morrison-strips-broadway-charity-show

http://television.aol.com/outside-the-box/glee/interview-with-matthew-morrison-chris-colfer-and-cory-monteith

http://thetvchick.com/exclusive-interviews/exclusive-interview-jayma-mays-emma-from-glee/

http://thetvchick.com/glee/interview-jessalyn-gilsig-terri-schuester-from-glee/

http://www.tv.com/video/19726/amber-riley-interview

http://www.tv.com/video/35302/glee--up-close-with-dianna-agron?o=tv

http://thetvaddict.com/2009/04/24/exclusive-interview-jane-lynch-talks-glee-and-party-down/

http://thetvaddict.com/2010/02/03/defying-hiatus-catching-up-with-glee-star-dianna-agron/

http://video.tvguide.com/Tonight+Show+With+Conan+OBrien/Chris+Colfer+Part+1/3167627

http://www.youngfatandfabulous.com/2009/10/exclusive-interview-with-amber-riley.html

http://www.younghollywood.com/vergetoemerge/cory-monteith.html

http://www.younghollywood.com/videos/tvfilm/tvfilm-events/introducingthe-cast-of-glee.html

http://www.younghollywood.com/videos/tvfilm/up-close/glee-heartthrob-mark-salling.html

http://www.youtube.com